D1596986

# A BRIEF HISTORY OF

# ST. JOHNSBURY

Peggy Pearl

# A BRIEF HISTORY OF
# ST. JOHNSBURY

PEGGY PEARL

THE
History
PRESS

Published by The History Press
Charleston, SC 29403
www.historypress.net

Copyright © 2009 by Peggy Pearl
All rights reserved

All images are courtesy of the author unless otherwise noted.

First published 2009

ISBN 978-1-5402-1885-8

Library of Congress Cataloging-in-Publication Data

Pearl, Peggy.
A brief history of St. Johnsbury / Peggy Pearl.
p. cm.
Includes bibliographical references and index.
ISBN 978-1-5402-1885-8
1. Saint Johnsbury (Vt.)--History. I. Title.
F59.S12P43 2009
974.3'34--dc22
2009026209

*Notice*: The information in this book is true and complete to the best of our knowledge. It is offered without guarantee on the part of the author or The History Press. The author and The History Press disclaim all liability in connection with the use of this book.

All rights reserved. No part of this book may be reproduced or transmitted in any form whatsoever without prior written permission from the publisher except in the case of brief quotations embodied in critical articles and reviews.

*To my parents, Lucia (Johnson) and William Pearl, with love for instilling in me a sense of place and values.*
*To my brothers, Tom and John, who will forever have a place in my heart.*
*To my sons, Thomas and Nicholas, in whom I hope I have instilled a sense of place.*
*To my sister, Elizabeth, who I am still working on to enjoy visiting and that history "stuff."*

# CONTENTS

# PREFACE

I sometimes make the remark that I was "brought up" in a cemetery owing to the fact that my father was superintendent of Mount Pleasant Cemetery and we lived in the house owned by the cemetery. I learned how to mow a lawn there, dig a grave (by hand) and also learned that there are definitely stories behind those stones. I return to these stones and stories throughout the book for the richness that they tell of the town's history.

What I hoped to accomplish with this brief history was a readable and enjoyable text. Somewhere, I hope there is a happy medium reached between historical facts and enjoyment.

# ACKNOWLEDGEMENTS

I would like to acknowledge posthumously those who have left behind their work of recording the town's history and laying the foundation for others to continue adding to the history. Thanks go to Edward Fairbanks, Arthur Stone, Claire Dunne Johnson, Gerald Heon, Graham Newell, Norman Atwood and George Crosby. Thanks also to early photographers and publishers of newspapers.

In the land of the living, thanks go to those who have shared stories of the town, especially my parents—Lucia and William Pearl. I would also thank Howard Reed for our many years of teaching, talking and sharing St. Johnsbury history. Thanks go to all who have shared sources and stories of St. Johnsbury.

Last but by no means least, thanks to two fellow classmates—Gaye Brown, who edits and has no time for tears but pushes you on! And Dianne Moulton Rolfe, who understands computers, their idiosyncrasies and abilities far better than I can ever hope for. Without their help, this would not have happened.

# CHAPTER 1

# WHAT'S IN A NAME?

Vermont declared itself an independent republic in 1777, thereby ending the claims of both New York and New Hampshire to its territory. Vermont became the fourteenth state in 1791. In November 1786, Governor Thomas Chittenden of Vermont granted a charter for the township of Saint Johnsbury, Vermont. This charter was issued to Dr. Jonathan Arnold. The township consisted of 21,167 acres, to be divided into 71 lots with approximately 310 acres each. The use of the name Saint Johnsbury was a first for a town and has remained that way—the only one in the world! How did the name come to be?

The trail leads back to a man by the name of Hector St. John de Crevecoeur, the French consul to the United States. He was born in Normandy, France, educated in England and came to Quebec in 1754, where he did military mapping for General Montcalm. He was young, and adventuring was in his blood. After exploration of the Great Lakes region and time spent in South Carolina and Nantucket, he decided to settle along the Hudson River on a large estate. Many readers may recognize him as the author of *Letters from an American Farmer*. In 1780, he returned to visit his homeland, and in 1783 he came back to the United States as the French consul. During this time, Ethan Allen, of the infamous Green Mountain Boys, had suggested that a Vermont town be named "St. John" after the French consul. In a letter to Allen in May 1885, Hector St. John wrote, "If the General don't think it too presumptuous, in order to answer what he so kindly said about names, I would observe that the name St. John being already given to so many places in this country, it might be contrived by the appellation of St. Johnsbury." A little over a year later, this name suggested by Hector St. John was applied to the township of St. Johnsbury. It is not duplicated in any other place in the world.

# Jonathan Arnold

As to Jonathan Arnold, the founder of St. Johnsbury, he was from Providence, Rhode Island, where his accomplishments had already earned him respect and honor. He had served as a surgeon in the Continental army during the Revolutionary War, with the rank of sergeant obtained. He was a member of the Continental Congress from Rhode Island from 1782 to 1784. He

Jonathan Arnold, founder of St. Johnsbury. *From* Town of St. Johnsbury, Vermont, *by Edward Fairbanks, 1914.*

had also authored and managed to get through the first declaration of independence from King George of England in 1776 for Rhode Island. His accomplishments might have made him an advocate for Vermont and its independent nature. History tells us that Jonathan Arnold had moved northward as far as Winchester, New Hampshire. A foundry established there lost him considerable money, which may have encouraged his journey to Vermont.

St. Johnsbury is two tiered, with the upper level now known as Main Street and a lower level known as Railroad Street. Early houses arose on the upper level, referred to as the Plain. As our history gets older and technology takes huge strides, it is often difficult for the current generation to grasp the full impact of early settlement. Who has experienced a true wilderness, with no stoves and no matches, and who would strike out today with an axe and maybe an ox, and otherwise only the possessions on your back? St. Johnsbury Plain was an unbroken wilderness when Jonathan Arnold and company arrived. In May 1787, Arnold, along with five others swinging axes, cleared and burned seven acres of forest in order to plant corn, potatoes, squash, beans and turnips in June. Legend has it that another ten acres were cleared the following month of July, in order to plant oats and wheat with clover mixed in. St. Johnsbury was on the map.

At the north end of the Plain, Jonathan Arnold constructed the first framed house in town. The small framed twenty-four- by thirty-square-foot house was constructed of sawn lumber from Arnold's up-and-down sawmill located on the Passumpsic River. It was a short distance from the building site on the lower level and was called Arnold's Falls. By 1840, the home had been abandoned and fallen into disrepair, and by daybreak of June 8, 1844, it had been reduced to ashes.

After this, the area was known as the Green and for about sixty years was an open space with no trees. Its uses included the starting place for horse races, a men's ball field, a meeting place for public assemblies under a tent and home of the first bandstand. In 1855, the space was fenced and trees were planted, and at this time it received the name Arnold Park, being part of the original homestead lot. More improvements were made in 1891, with approximately four hundred loads of dirt dumped there and graded. A fountain from the Mott Iron Works of New York was erected by citizens of the vicinity at a cost of $400. The style is the "Gargoyle Octagon Pan with Vase Bearer" with a height to the top of the pan of seven feet and a total height of eleven feet, seven inches. Several streams of water flow from the pan through goats' heads into the ground basin, the pan being replenished by jets of water that come out of the vase that the "bearer" holds over her head. The laying out

Fountain at Arnold Park.

of another path or two with the location of a few seats completed the work of 1891. The committee that did the solicitation and procuring of the fountain included E.T. Ide, Doctor H.S. Browne and S.A. Nelson. Two oak trees on the north side of the park were planted by Colonel George Chamberlain before he left for the Civil War. In 1898, the fencing was removed. The Dutch elm disease took its toll on the trees in the park, as it did to the whole of Main Street, in the mid-1900s. Once again, the fountain needs attention as the weather has taken a toll on "the Lady," as she is affectionately called today. The original cost of $400 in 1891 has been inflated to $51,000 in 2009 for the repairs by a Boston-based iron restoration company. Signs are up in the park indicating the monetary progress, and residents of St. Johnsbury will be sure to dig deeper in their pockets to preserve "the Lady."

## Mount Pleasant Cemetery

The graves of the Arnold family may be found at Mount Pleasant Cemetery, having been moved from the Old Burial Ground (where the courthouse is now) in the 1850s. As you enter from the Mount Pleasant Street entrance and take the road to the far left up the hill, they are located under the pines near the iron fence. Looking at the family lot, the next stone to the right marks the grave of the Negro slave of the Arnold family, Ruth Farrow. She came from Rhode Island with the Arnold family. She was given her freedom by Jonathan Arnold when slavery was abolished in Rhode Island, but she chose to remain with the family. She lived fifty-three years in St. Johnsbury, serving three generations of the Arnold family. She was known to many village children as Aunt Ruth. This story was put in poetry by Charles H. Horton of St. Johnsbury and goes like this:

*The Pioneer and the Slave*

*Side by side in a narrow lot,*
*In a quiet unfrequented spot,*
*Are two most unassuming graves,*
*The pioneer's—the faithful slave's.*

*One marble slab, white, cut with care,*
*And one of slate, dark, low and bare.*
*Save but one name—stand o'er these graves,*
*The pioneer's—the faithful slave's.*

*And yet how well they symbolize*
*The master's and the servant's lives;*
*One, white, high-born, both free and brave,*
*One, dark, in bondage born, a slave.*

Monuments to Jonathan Arnold and family and Ruth Farrow in Mount Pleasant Cemetery.

*Yet both did serve—both slaves were they,*
*And both a master did obey;*
*Each in their lives exemplified*
*The true slave spirit 'till they died.*

*But in his varied tasks great deeds*
*One saw; he served his nation's needs;*
*And to great principles was nerved,*
*And one knew only that she served.*

*Side by side in these quiet graves*
*Long buried lie these faithful slaves;*
*Both servants to eternal plans*
*Yet one served God's, the other man's.*

## Early Settlers

In Zadock Thompson's 1842 *History of Vermont*, St. Johnsbury is geographically described: "St. Johnsbury, a post town in the eastern part of Caledonia county, is in lat. 44o27' and long. 4o58', and is bounded northerly by Lyndon, northeast by Kirby, southeast by Waterford, and southwest by Danville." In this described area, and prior to this charter being issued to Jonathan Arnold, there were already inhabitants. The Adams family (James, Martin, Jonathan and James Calendar Adams) were the first settlers of St. Johnsbury, and other early settlers' names included two Trescott brothers, Jonathan and William, and Thomas Todd, Benjamin Doolittle, Josiah Nichols and Simeon Cole. They were granted one hundred acres each on the area where they had "landed."

Of these earliest inhabitants, Jonathan Trescott may have gained more notoriety in death than in life. He, too, spent his first years of burial at the Old Burial Ground (where the courthouse is now) on the Plain. He died in 1848 at the age of eighty-eight; in 1856, his body was disinterred for reburial at Mount Pleasant Cemetery. His body was said to have been completely solidified and was heavier than four men could lift. Jonathan became known as "the petrified man" in later articles that appeared in the *Caledonian* newspaper of 1864—the correspondent was known only as "C." Hiram Cutting of Lunenburg, Vermont, sought to explain this phenomenon as not being truly petrified but the formation of adipocere. All of this resulted in Jonathan Trescott being exhumed again on June 3, 1864. Cutting found "the body of Mr. Trescott not petrified but in a remarkable state of preservation," according to the *Caledonian* of June 10, 1864. Once again, Jonathan was laid to rest and has remained so these many years.

Land in St. Johnsbury in 1787 was advertised for a dollar an acre; twenty dollars in hard money paid down on one hundred acres; another fifty dollars in neat cattle in six months and the balance due within eighteen months, consisting of thirty dollars in grain or neat stock or as the grain was produced. "Neat stock" is an old term that refers to cows or oxen. This advertised land brought further immigration from southern New England, including southern New Hampshire, Connecticut, Rhode Island and parts of Massachusetts. When looking at old maps of St. Johnsbury, you will see names that represented certain named areas, such as the Hawkins and Goss names for the Goss Hollow area located in the upper branches of the Sleepers River; Spaulding Neighborhood to the east of the Village. Wheeler, Roberts, Ayer, Pierce and Sanger were some of the early setters following the chartering of the town.

A real plus for St. Johnsbury was the abundance of water in the three rivers coming through. The Passumpsic flows north to south, where it is joined by the Moose coming in from the northeast. The Sleepers River comes in from the northwest. Water power was readily available within the town of St. Johnsbury, which set the stage for the future settlement and development.

# EARLY SETTLEMENT AND INDUSTRY

The first census of the United States in 1790 recorded for "St. Johnsbury, Town, county of Orange (now Caledonia)," 34 families consisting of 143 people. The breakdown of this number was 54 men, 55 women and girls and 34 boys under sixteen years of age. At this time St. Johnsbury's population compared to Danville's 574, Peacham's 365 and Barnet's 477.

Although the charter was granted in 1786 to Jonathan Arnold, the first official town meeting was not held until 1790. Major concerns were for monetary support from the legislature for bridges and roads. Another issue that kept coming to the floor at these early meetings was compensation for a minister and a meetinghouse. The raising of this meetinghouse took place in the summer of 1804. The contract for the building that was to serve as the place for town meetings as well as religious meetings was given to Captain John Stiles and Nahum Stiles, and the structure was to be erected on a piece of land given by Thomas Pierce. The location was approximately a half mile west from the Center Village. Looking at the map of St. Johnsbury, the center was just about central for everybody. At the raising of the meetinghouse, the duties of the men and boys was to raise the timbers and the women and girls to feed, cheer on the raisers and mix the toddy. The event of raising the meetinghouse was capped off by one of the raisers. Zibe Tute balanced on his head at the end of the ridge pole of this sixty-two- by forty-four-foot structure, "swallow[ed] the contents of his flask, and descend[ed] head downwards to the ground." For forty-one years, the building stood on this high ground, but in 1845 it was taken down and re-erected where it now stands as the First Congregational Church in the Center Village next to the little cemetery. The original site is marked by a granite monument just off exit 22 of I-91.

The original meetinghouse after it had been moved to the Center Village.

## Industry and Mills

Industry, however, was not as methodical as the democracy of the town, so the harnessing of the Passumpsic River began. Jonathan Arnold set up the first sawmill in 1787 on the lower level, just a short distance from his homesite. For many years, the mill site was called Arnold Falls and provided lumber for many homes built on the Plain. A year later, a gristmill was established and run by the brother of Jonathan. Next, David Bowen took over the gristmill and built the first rather crude house in that area. Further development at Arnold Falls came with the arrival of Captain James Ramsey in 1817. He took over the gristmill, added a small building into which he moved his family, and set up a carding machine. In 1820, Ramsey and Allen Kent put up a larger and better sawmill at the falls. Approximately three years later, the mill was bought by Hiram Jones and Sargent Bagley, who also built a carpenter shop beside the mill. Ramsey manufactured spinning wheels that were considered superior. The following was an ad:

*Improved Patent Accelerating Wheel Head $1.13 each*
*Manufactured by James Ramsey*
*Cast Steel Set in Brass*
*Will Require Frequent Oiling*

*Spinning Wheels of every kind;*
*Quilling Wheels, reels, shuttles,*
*And Spools may be had at the*
*Shop in St. Johnsbury, Caledonia County, Vermont*
*All warranted good or no sale.*

This Ramsey manufacturing brick building still stands beside the Passumpsic River today; it presently houses a restaurant. Ramsey built a brick house a little south of the bridge. Known as an abolitionist, Ramsey's home, prior to the Civil War, harbored runaway slaves and helped them escape to Canada. In doing so, his house was part of the Underground Railroad and the only known underground station in town. The Arnold Falls name gave way to Ramsey's Mills. A remembrance of James Ramsey by a boy at the time was that of a "character, a large, bony Scotchman, with a fund of droll stories which he delighted to tell to the neighbors and over which he would shake with laughter." In later years, the Ramseys would lose their son John in the Civil War at the Battle of Savage Station, Virginia, in 1862.

In 1818, Huxham Paddock had a trip hammer and iron foundry on the Sleepers River. His contract for water power called for enough to carry one trip hammer, one grindstone and two pairs of bellows. In 1828, he moved his operation to Arnold Falls. The Paddock Iron Works set up a blast furnace and machine shop to grow the ironworks. A large workforce was employed as the business grew and many of these workers built homes nearby, where the name changed again to Paddock Village. Teams of oxen or horses would bring in ores from Franconia, New Hampshire. Lesser amounts were obtained from Piermont, New Hampshire, and Waterford and Troy, Vermont. Fuel was obtained from nearby woods, and the superior quality of iron made here by combining these ores was used in the production of stoves and hollow ironware. A remembered piece of equipment was a turning lathe capable of turning a shaft of three feet in diameter and fourteen feet in length. It was probably recorded because it rivaled anything else in the state of Vermont.

The same mill development was happening farther up the Passumpsic in the Center Village. Eleazar Sanger put a dam up and established an up-and-down sawmill. Reuben Spaulding ran the first gristmill, followed by Enoch Wing. A story of Enoch's tenure as the miller tells of the increasing need for the mill in the fall, prompting round-the-clock grinding. Enoch would fill the hoppers at night and then lie down beside the stones as they did the grinding. When they had no grain, the stones made a different sound, which awoke Enoch and then he would refill the hoppers and begin again—both grinding and napping!

Paddock Village.

Meanwhile, the Sleepers River was being harnessed in the Goss Hollow area of St. Johnsbury. David Goss started with a sawmill in 1793, which was followed by a gristmill, blacksmith shop, starch factory and wool-carding and cloth-dressing mill. Add to this a harness-making and saddle shop and Goss Hollow was a thriving hamlet for a time.

East Village was utilizing the Moose River with two dams. A gristmill was operated in 1800 by Mr. Fowler. The year 1830 saw a carding factory established by Silas Hubbard. The Smith brothers had a starch factory, and a tannery was established by Franklin Griswold. Hill's cider mill was a popular place for many a year. These early individuals harnessed the Passumpsic, the Sleepers and the Moose Rivers to provide for their homes, food and businesses.

A view of East St. Johnsbury.

## Mount Pleasant Cemetery

Returning to Mount Pleasant Cemetery, you can find three of these early settlers and their families. Heading straight out into the cemetery from the chapel, with the towering spruce as your marker, stop just below the terrace that the tree rises from and face the Belknap family's granite monument. Buried here are three generations of very talented hands. Amos arrived from New Hampshire about 1824 and apprenticed blacksmithing under Samuel Crossman for seven years. He then set up shop on the Sleepers River in the South Main Street area. Amos is remembered for his edge tools; it is recorded that he would make as many as three hundred axes in a year. Close inspections of knives that have survived show not only a fine edge but also brass work joining the edge to the handle in equally fine craftsmanship.

John was one of two sons who followed in their father Amos's footsteps, and his abilities took many directions, from that of knife blades to finely crafted rifles. Knife blades were turned out at nearly one hundred a week and were sold for twenty-five cents each. It would be worth checking any old jackknife to see if the Belknap name was at the base. John also manufactured water motors, one of his first powering the *Caledonian* press. John's life was cut short, for on his gravestone it reads that he was drowned at the age of forty-eight years. This tragedy occurred in late November 1888 on the Passumpsic River opposite the current State Police Barracks on Route 5, south of the village. A dam had been completed, which had been a longtime idea of John's, having bought the water privilege earlier that year. With others, he had organized the Water Power Company, and everything was in place, with the water going over the dam for the first time that day. John was helping to secure a timber about twenty-five feet in length that was afloat above the dam. The timber was caught by the current, swung around and carried John and the boat he was in over the dam. John called for a rope, but the current swept him away before he could be rescued.

The third generation of Belknaps was John's son, Harry, who inherited his father's mechanical abilities. He was seventeen at the time of his father's death, which he witnessed. Upon his father's death, he entered W.C. Warner's store to learn the watchmaker's trade. Harry worked in Lowell, Massachusetts, for a short time and then returned to St. Johnsbury and manufactured rings and watches out of his home on Railroad Street. At the time of his death at the young age of thirty-two, he owned a block on Railroad Street and had built up a large trade in the watch, jewelry and optical business. The abilities of these three generations of Belknaps could be summed up in the words of one of the ads that Henry ran in the St. Johnsbury Directory of 1897–98, which reads in part, "Some people talk with their mouths, others with their fingers. We talk through our goods."

Next door to the Belknap lot we find the Hubbard Lawrence family. If one were to search the cemetery stones over for words of perfection of a departed soul, you would end up here:

*Deac. Hubbard Lawrence*
*an affectionate Husband.*
*a faithful Father. an exemplary Christian.*
*an officer of the Church & a*
*valuable Member of society.*
*died Sept. 20, 1816*
*aged 43 years*
*leaving a wid$^{ow}$ & 9 children*
*Think mortals what it is to die.*

Lawrence ran a tannery on what is now Western Avenue, former site of Pinehurst, home of Horace Fairbanks and now the Elks' home. Town records indicate that Ralph Merry operated a tannery as early as 1795. He sold it to Philip Bean in 1797, and Hubbard Lawrence bought it about 1802. Leather was all important for crafting harnesses, saddles, shoes, boots, aprons, belts, slings from which a coach body hung and many other items. Recorded early

Hubbard Lawrence
Stone.

history says that Hubbard marked his hides with a *G* or a *B*—representing good or bad quality. In 2008, a bit of history was unearthed. While trying to divert water on the lawn of the Elks Home, workers discovered four boxes beneath the sod. They were surrounded by blue clay and had what appeared to be peat now but would originally have been bark in them. Three were approximately eight feet in length, eighteen to twenty-four inches wide, with a like depth. This evidence certainly points to a tannery, as a tannery used lots of water, vats were sunk to ground level and separated by walkways and a tan vat was often described with an approximate length of six feet, four feet deep and four to six feet wide. This discovery is a true testament to endurance, as the tannery ceased operating about 1830. Hubbard served his community well, including being a leader in the first meetinghouse in the center. He was the moderator and a chosen deacon. Lawrence and David Stowell were responsible for sustaining the public worship, for it was to be six years before a pastor could be had. Mrs. (Mary) Lawrence stood on equal ground with her husband, then widowed with nine children. In Edward Fairbank's *History of St. Johnsbury*, he quotes the memory of Milo Jewett in 1820 of the widow Lawrence (whose home was on lower Main Street near the old burial ground): "My childhood recollection of Mrs. Lawrence brings her before me as a model woman, a type of all that is strong and noble and sweet in womanhood and in full sympathy with childhood. However noisy or rude our sports, she was always patient, carrying an air of authority tempered with gentleness."

Milo grew up in the Jewett-Ide House just south of the Paddock house. Jewett was a graduate of Dartmouth College and Andover Theological Seminary. He became friends with Matthew Vassar in 1856 and convinced him to convert the Cottage Hill Seminary in Poughkeepsie, New York, into America's first college for women. Doctor Milo P. Jewett was appointed first president of Vassar College.

## Other Early Industries

Another early establishment was the St. Johnsbury Stone Ware Pottery begun by Major Richard Fenton in 1808. The location of the low red buildings was west of the Passumpsic River and half a mile south of the Center Village. Power was provided by a brook that made its way down a hillside. Until tinware became available, the demand for this pottery was constant. Leander, the son of Richard, operated this business until it was destroyed by fire in November 1859. Richard's brother, Christopher, is the potter associated with the pottery works in Bennington, Vermont. A printed price list survived, issued by L. Fenton, "manufacturer of every kind of stone ware." The variety included jugs, pots, churns, pitchers, butter pots, bean pots, spittoons, mugs, etc. Prices were by the dozen, which would suggest wholesale and perhaps beyond the St. Johnsbury area. Two gallon churns were listed at $4.50 a dozen and pint jars were $0.75 a dozen. An occasional piece of this early pottery can still be found in homes or antique shops.

Two other early industries should be noted, the first being that of potash or pearl ash. This is often referred to as the first cash crop in Vermont, and there were several potasheries in St. Johnsbury. As forests were cut down, trees that were not used in building were burned. The ashes were collected and slowly leached with water, which produced lye. The water in the lye was boiled out, leaving a gray, dry powder called potash. John and Luther Clark operated a potasherie right on the Plain between the St. Johnsbury House and the church (present site of the Colonial Apartments). There was a rather large gulley that extended across the Plain in that very area that had a footbridge. Another potasherie known as Phelps Potash existed near the head of the Plain.

The second early industry was that of brick making. Samuel French had a brickyard in the center of town. The Bagley brickworks were started in 1810 near the Paddock Village area. Samuel's son Ira, born here in 1813, continued making bricks throughout his lifetime. He made all the brick in the original courthouse, the first Catholic church on Cherry Street and the Athenaeum.

An unidentified handwritten description of the Plain reads like this:

> *Description of St. Johnsbury Plain*
> *St. Johnsbury Plain is very pleasantly situated about two miles and a half south from the centre of the town: it has a free circulation of air, the land sloping each way from the Plain in every direction except at the North West part where it rises to a considerable heighth above a prospect from which is very delightful. The Hotel stands about centre of the Plain from North to South; it is at present occupied by Mr. Rice under whose care it is managed so that it gains the patronage of the public: on the Plain there several very pleasant dwelling houses, on the South part of the Plain there are two shoemakers shops, two tailoresses, three Hatters shops, one blacksmith shop and tannery there is also two practicing Physicians and a Minister.*
>
> *On the North part of the Plain there is one Cabinet makers shop, two English Westindies & American good stores, one Millinner and mantamaker* [mantua—a loose gown open in front to reveal an underskirt, worn in the seventeenth and eighteenth centuries (from the *American Heritage Dictionary of the English Language*)] *and one saddler and harness maker, there is also one Attorney at law: the pats* [maybe post] *office is near the North end of the Plain kept in a lawyers office at which four different mails arrive and depart twice a week, there a District school, a female Academy and a musick school. A new and elegant Meeting houss is shortly to be completed about twenty rods North of the Hotel. It is to contain an organ and when finished it is hoped and expected will add much to the well being of society.*

The above description was probably written about 1850 with the mention of the Hotel. The St. Johnsbury House was an answer to demand for better hotel accommodations due to the coming of the railroad. The hotel had

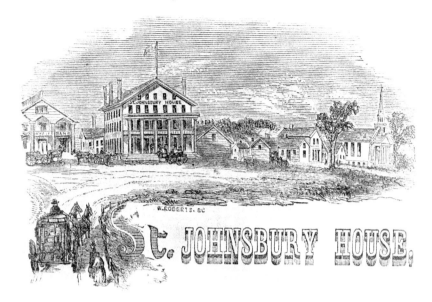

St. Johnsbury House and early Plain layout. *Courtesy of Gerald Heon.*

150 rooms and could accommodate two hundred guests. Its hospitality was praised as a reason to stop in St. Johnsbury while traveling.

Before we advance further in the development of St. Johnsbury, we must bring in the Fairbanks family, for they were most influential in shaping the town's growth in the fields of manufacture, both intellectually and culturally.

# CHAPTER 3

# FAIRBANKS ERA

On May 20, 1815, Joseph and Phoebe Paddock Fairbanks left Brimfield, Massachusetts, for St. Johnsbury, Vermont. He was the sixth generation from Jonathan Fairbanks from Yorkshire, England. Jonathan came over in 1633 and built the Fairbanks House, still standing in Dedham, Massachusetts. Joseph and Phoebe had a farm in Brimfield after moving from Sherburne, Massachusetts, the birthplace of Joseph. Questions are often asked by St. Johnsbury inhabitants and visitors about the Fairbanks genealogy, so this brief lineage is included. How was it that the Fairbanks family headed north?

One name that should ring a bell from the previous chapter is Paddock. Phoebe's brother was Ephraim Paddock, who had come north on foot from Holland, Massachusetts, in 1780. He was both pupil and instructor at Peacham Academy; he then entered a law office in Danville, was admitted to the bar and began practice in St. Johnsbury in 1807. In 1828, he was elected to the supreme court of Vermont. It was the encouragement of Ephraim through letters that drew the Fairbanks to St. Johnsbury. In 1820, Ephraim and Abba had the first brick home built in town. Set back from the main street, it expressed dignity then and now. The brick was made on the grounds by bricklayers from Connecticut under the supervision of William Gage of Walpole, New Hampshire. The blinds and parts of the wood finish were hand made by their nephew, Thaddeus Fairbanks. The Bay of Naples wallpaper still hangs on the parlor walls. This home had two other firsts: the first piano in town, played by the Paddocks' daughter, Charlotte, and the start of the St. Johnsbury Female Academy. Sessions were held in the southwest chamber of the house from 1825 until the Academy moved south on the Plain.

Joseph and Phoebe arrived in St. Johnsbury with two of their sons, Thaddeus and Joseph. The older son, Erastus, was already in the area. They

Paddock House.

took up residence near the Sleepers River on five acres that included rights to the falls. The price paid was $300. First up and running was the sawmill in the fall of 1815, followed by the gristmill in the spring of 1816. The upper floor of the gristmill had machinery for making wagons, and by the spring of 1817, at the age of twenty-one, Thaddeus was turning out several pleasure wagons. The gristmill, along with the wagon machinery, was washed away in a flood of 1828.

Thaddeus had an inventive mind that would go "clickity clack" right up until he turned ninety years old. Wagon-making was followed by the construction of a small iron foundry in 1823, where he manufactured cast-iron plows and stoves. A patent was obtained in 1826 for the cast-iron plow, followed two years later by an invention of a box stove with a "diving flue." Arthur Stone, in an article in the *Caledonian*, quotes the announcement of this stove: "By means of the rising flue and rolling damper, the draft is increased to any desirable degree, and the oven, which is large, is easily tempered at the will of the user and is never liable to burn or scorch."

## E. & T. Fairbanks Company

In 1824, Erastus joined his brother Thaddeus in the manufacturing of these plows, stoves, pitchforks and hoes. From this union began the E. & T.

Fairbanks Company, which would next address the hemp craze that entered the area. In the late 1820s, there was a demand for hemp, which was needed in the making of rope. Many farmers turned parts of their land over for growing this crop. A machine for dressing hemp had been patented in 1826 by J. Haines of New York. The E. & T. Fairbanks Company built three of these Haines machines for the purpose of dressing local hemp. The size alone of these machines is worth noting, as they were thirty-two feet long and four feet in width and included sixty-five pairs of fluted rollers that geared together for the purpose of breaking the hempstraw as it passed between the rollers. Thaddeus was responsible for making the gear wheels and the machine for fluting the rollers. During this time, he received a patent on an improved hemp dresser and was the manager of the St. Johnsbury Hemp Company. This venture was short-lived, but out of it would come the longtime success of the E. & T. Fairbanks Company.

Hemp was delivered by the wagonload and valued at that time around fifteen dollars a ton. Weighing a wagonload of hemp by the old method of a steelyard and chains was not only awkward but also highly inaccurate. Thaddeus turned his attention to bettering this method of weighing, and the result would be known as the platform scale. Its success was measured

## WAGGONS & SLEIGHS.

THE Subscriber would inform his friends and the public that he continues the manufacturing of

*WAGGONS & SLEIGHS*

of various descriptions, at his stand near St. Johnsbury Plain. Having obtained the best of white oak timber for every part of his work where it is necessary, he pledges himself that the work and materials cannot fail to suit the purchaser.

T. FAIRBANKS.

*St. Johnsbury, Jan.* 28, 1819.

N. B. Those who wish for Pleasure Waggons may have them hung on leather, so as to convey the rider much easier than in Chaise. Single Waggons are generally kept on hand.

An advertisement for wagons and sleighs. *Courtesy of Fairbanks Museum.*

The Fairbanks factory in 1830. *Courtesy of Fairbanks Museum.*

by the fact that it would go on to weigh the world. His initial design was to rest a platform on two long levers that were connected to a steelyard, upon which a counterbalance was placed. No longer did the wagon have to be precariously suspended, and the weight seemed to be accurate. Thaddeus was not quite satisfied and took his plan another step forward; by adding two short levers to his long ones, he had support points at all four corners. Durability, stability and accuracy were achieved with this design. The Fairbanks brothers probably did not foresee the importance of what they had created, for their thought was that maybe a few towns would opt to buy platform scales for weighing hay. By 1833, Joseph P., the third and youngest brother, had joined the growing company, assuming the role of salesman.

The first platform scales were made of wood and were introduced to the public as town hay scales in Vermont. This was only the beginning, as Thaddeus's principal invention was developed into portable platform, warehouse and counter scales. These were followed by livestock, railroad track, canal, druggist and postal scales. From one-tenth of a grain to tons would be weighed using Thaddeus's invention. The first scales were produced in a wooden shop 25 by 60 feet with 1,500 square feet of floor space. It was a combination of a factory, warehouse and salesroom all in one.

Many years later, Thaddeus wrote down some of his remembrances of those early scale days:

My plans were all made in the night, frequently working nearly all night. For lack of tools, the scale work all had to be finished by hand, and this, with work on the patterns, etc. required all my time during the day in the shops. Faulty work was sure to be sent out unless I was watching all the time; men had to be educated to do the simplest things; there was no uniform machine work as now; it was fifteen years before we had a planer in the shop. In the south end of the old red shop Mr. Levi Fuller and I made the platform scale patterns from the number 1 to 10, also in the west end of the grist mill chamber the number one and two iron lever hay scales. Our casting was done in a shed annexed to the old forge; we were still in want of funds, but a larger building was finally put up; it developed on me to put in the cupola and fixtures, blast, etc., and start operations. I moulded and took the melting often; there was no other way to learn what made the unsound stogy places and air blisters; in order to teach the men how to make sound castings I had to work several months mixing metals and testing their composition.

In making plans for scales I found three things to be considered—the strength of material, the best shape to secure greatest strength with least material, and the beauty and symmetry of outside appearance. To imagine what the tastes and notions of men in reference to the right proportioning and beauty of this new article would be, was difficult; but now after the lapse of fifty years our platform scales are made precisely after the original design, and all other makers follow the same.

A Fairbanks Scales sales card.

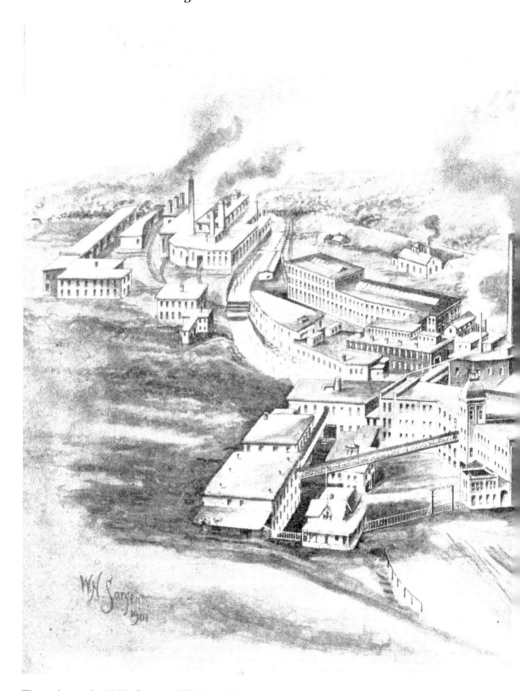

The scales works, 1906. *Courtesy of Fairbanks Museum.*

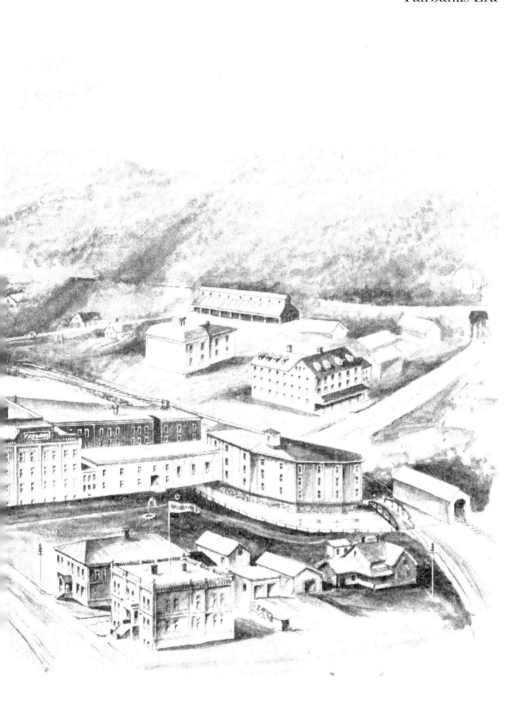

Contrast these early recollections by Thaddeus and the size of the original building with an article in the *Scientific American* of November 6, 1880:

> *Ten substantial brick buildings, with nearly ten acres of floor room, now take the place of the original shop; there is also a lumber yard covering ten acres, in which are constantly kept from two to three million feet of lumber; there are over 600 men employed, and 93 tenement houses for the employees; the capital invested now amounts to over $2,000,000, and the annual product to considerably more than that, while in 1831 it was less than $6,000.*

The patterns made by Thaddeus and Levi Fuller in 1831 now occupied a separate building, thirty-two by eighty feet and two stories high. Sending out only the best in goods, they beat out cheaper-made scales and were, at this time, the largest manufacturer of scales in the world.

The May 26, 1887 edition of the St. Johnsbury newspaper, the *Caledonian*, presented a bird's-eye view of the scale works. It was reported that the scale business was sharing in the upward business movement in the country. An addition to the machine shops was being built—sixty-eight by seventy feet and three stories high. On June 15, it was reported the new "envelope" system of paying off at the scale works went into operation: "Each man now receives at his bench an envelope, on the outside of which is a statement of the amount earned, deductions for rent, store account, etc., while inside is the balance due. The piece hands appreciate the new scheme as it saves valuable time."

In a September edition reporting on the annual meeting of September 14, a total of 625 men were employed in the shops. They were finishing about 1,500 scales a week, which left them about 5,000 orders behind. In the October 27 edition, the production of scales for the previous week reached an all-time high of over 1,600.

A glimpse of what a presence the scale works had in the town was reflected in a talk given by William Pearl in March 1987, recalling growing up on Cliff Street in the 1920s–30s:

> *Cliff Street, in the days of the 1920's and the 1930's was dominated by the Fairbanks Company. The great steam gong bellowed out of the Fairbanks Village, morning, noon and night...It was not a sound that filled you with apprehension. It made you realize that men had a place to go to work, that it was a sustaining force on the community. You could hear that gong in Danville and it was a paramount sound in St. Johnsbury*

*for many, many years. It called men to work; some who spent a relatively short time there, some a long time and some a working lifetime. The men went down the street. They walked to work. They were not faceless images behind a tinted windshield.*

# Mount Pleasant Cemetery

Returning to Mount Pleasant Cemetery, if monuments could speak, there would be many that would bear testimony to "a working lifetime" at Fairbanks. Taking the road to the left of the chapel and heading up the hill until the road forks, bearing right and looking on the right, you find the name Walker. Perhaps Colonel Francis Walker would hold the record for longevity, as he entered the employ of the Fairbanks Company in October 1845, learning the trade of a moulder. He retired on March 1, 1910, after sixty years at the head of the foundry. The title "Colonel" was complimentary, given him by his many friends. He entered at a time when stoves, plows, forks, hoes and scales were being made and earned $100 a year for the first two years. What a story lies behind that stone. His resting place looks down on those who were his Fairbanks bosses for so many years.

The partnership of the three Fairbanks brothers was indeed unique, with each bringing sound values, good work ethics and compassion for those who worked for them. Knowing that the E. & T. Fairbanks Company flourished under the leadership of the three brothers, one might expect to see some rather prominent gravestones to indicate their success in life. Their plots are a bit larger due to family members buried there, but their stones fit right in with the tanner and blacksmith. You would use the same spruce tree that got you to the Belknap and Lawrence stones, straight out from the chapel, to find generations of the Fairbanks family.

Erastus Fairbanks and family are located directly across from the Belknap lot (the terrace just below where the spruce tree rises). A white marble monument with inscriptions that have faded over the years speaks to Erastus and Lois Crossman of Peacham. Erastus was the oldest of the three sons born to Joseph and Phoebe (Paddock) Fairbanks on October 28, 1792. Erastus came north from Brimfield, Massachusetts, before the rest of his family. He was to study law with his Uncle Ephraim Paddock, but poor eyesight forced him to give up on that endeavor. He taught school for a time and then turned his interests to the mercantile business, first in Wheelock and finally in Barnet before returning to St. Johnsbury and entering into business with Thaddeus. He was at the head of the firm for thirty years.

Foundry crew. Francis Walker is in the second row, the fifth seated man from the left. *Courtesy of William Pearl.*

Erastus also became prominent in public life. Politics saw him a member of the Whig Party, and after that party dissolved he became a Republican. In 1836, he represented St. Johnsbury in the state legislature, a position that he held for the next three years. He was elected to serve as the governor of Vermont twice: once in 1852 and again in 1860 at the outbreak of the Civil War. At this time, the state placed $1 million at his disposal, to be spent relying solely on his judgment. He did not draw a salary during this time as governor. He played a very important role in getting the railroad this far north, and when the Passumpsic and Connecticut Rivers Railroad Corporation was formed in 1849, Erastus was chosen its president.

He was an officer and member of the North Congregational Church, setting a fine example of religious belief and honesty in his personal and business life. For forty-nine years he shared his life with Lois Crossman, with nine children being born to that union. He lived to be seventy-two years old, dying in 1864. No accolades are on his monument.

Thaddeus's family lot is beyond the spruce and to the right. It has a granite border with steps to enter the actual lot. It is sheltered by evergreen trees and makes no mention of his successes in life. Even before his successful scale, Thaddeus was inventing and making things, including the wagon that brought the family to St. Johnsbury. Thaddeus was in the business for fifty-five years as inventor of not only the original scale but also modifications of scales to come and machines to make the scale parts. He secured thirty-two patents following the original platform scale.

He also took a very active interest in the good of the whole of St. Johnsbury. In 1842, the three brothers founded St. Johnsbury Academy. From 1866 to 1882, all expenses of the Academy were paid by Thaddeus. He was an active trustee of the Academy board until his death. Middlebury and Dartmouth Colleges were both recipients of his generosity with various scholarships.

Thaddeus was a member of the South Congregational Church, giving the organ and remodeling the church in 1876 at his own expense. In 1873, he was made a knight of the Order of Francis Joseph by the emperor of Austria, which led to his affectionately being called "Sir Thaddeus" by the townspeople. Lucy Peck Barker was his wife from 1820 until her death in 1866. To them were born five children, with three dying in infancy.

One other patent that Thaddeus received that bears mentioning is that of a refrigerator in 1856 based on the principle of placing the ice above the food cabinet, thus allowing a down-flow of dry, cool air. He had neither the time nor money to pursue this patent, so he gave up his rights, which were later valued close to $1 million! Always the inventor, his last patent was for an improved "feed water heater," issued February 23, 1886—just prior to his ninetieth birthday year. It would also be the year of his passing.

Joseph, the father, and Joseph P., the brother, are located on the same terrace as Thaddeus, and again there are no words of their accomplishments. Joseph P. was the youngest brother, born in 1806. He was but a young boy as they journeyed north from Brimfield, Massachusetts, in 1815. Along with brother Erastus, the businessman, and Thaddeus, the inventor, Joseph might be labeled the intellect and salesman.

In 1825, young men of St. Johnsbury formed a literary society called St. Johnsbury Philadelphian Society, of which Joseph was an active member. Like his brother Erastus, he too commenced the study of law with his Uncle Ephraim in 1826. After his admission to the bar, he practiced with his uncle and then opened his own office. In less than three years, he too chose to enter the mercantile business in Troy, Vermont, with his cousin, Horace Paddock. He closed that business after a year and joined with his brothers in 1833. In a letter, Joseph wrote, "The reason of my leaving is because my brothers have made me proposals so tempting that I cannot resist—which are the privileges of riding about the country and peddling out Hay Scales." His territory was Maine, and he established himself

ERASTUS FAIRBANKS                    THADDEUS FAIRBANKS
            JOSEPH PADDOCK FAIRBANKS
    HORACE FAIRBANKS            FRANKLIN FAIRBANKS
        BUILDERS OF THE SCALE INDUSTRY

Two generations of Fairbanks men. *From* Town of St. Johnsbury, Vermont, *by Edward Fairbanks, 1914.*

in Waterville. By 1839, his brothers prevailed upon him to return to St. Johnsbury, where he conducted extensive correspondence for the business and oversaw most of the operations abroad.

He also saw public service and was elected to the state legislature in 1845, where he was dedicated to the improvement of public schools. After a business trip to Cuba in 1847, which saw months of travel, he returned home with health problems. He was a trustee of Middlebury College as well as the first president of the Passumpsic Bank. His other interest was that of agriculture, and he wrote articles encouraging men to stay in Vermont and develop agricultural resources here rather than to join the movement west.

He encouraged his brothers to promote the improvement of men employed by the company through the establishment of a library and reading room. He delivered lectures to them, had the employees do the same and even offered prizes for the best work. Joseph's marriage to Almira Taylor bore two sons, William and Edward. In 1855, Joseph and his son Edward went on a business trip to St. Louis. He became very ill, returning in mid-April, and died May 15. Although his life was short, he was able to succeed in many ways.

Three generations of Fairbanks left their imprint on St. Johnsbury. It started with their settlement on the Sleepers River, beginning with a sawmill. The depth of the print increased with the invention of Thaddeus's platform scale and a very successful business that saw growth in the town's education, religion and culture. Their legacy had beneficial roots for all to enjoy now and into the foreseeable future. Their legacy will be explored in Chapter 5.

# CHAPTER 4

# DEVELOPMENT OF RAILROAD STREET

The year 1850 was a year of development. The first major expansion on the Plain (Main Street) took shape with the laying out of Summer Street, running parallel to Main on the west side. It was the year that Eastern Avenue connected Railroad to Main Street. And the big news was the coming of trains to St. Johnsbury in 1850. Railroad Street was new and open for business.

It should be noted that prior to the arrival of the railroad, everything came and went to its destination by horse and ox teams. St. Johnsbury was landlocked as far as transportation was concerned. All farm produce and manufactured goods were hauled to and from Boston or Portland, Maine—the two major markets at the time. Imagine being the teamster when the trip to Boston and back took perhaps three to four weeks. The distance to Portland was shorter, approximately five days one way. Loads of iron ore and pig iron (partially processed iron) were hauled from Franconia for use in the Paddock and Fairbanks businesses. Thousands of tons of this iron were required to be hauled by very heavy teams for these two businesses. The needs of the Fairbanks scale works secured the coming of the trains.

## Railroad

The Connecticut and Passumpsic Rivers Railroad Company was headed by Erastus Fairbanks. This line ran north from the mouth of the White River to St. Johnsbury and continued on to Newport. Twenty and a half miles of grading and masonry, from Wells River to St. Johnsbury, were begun January 23, 1850, and completed in November of the same year. During that time period, forty-five thousand cubic yards of rock had to be blasted and one million cubic yards excavated. On November 18, 1850, the construction

Eastern Avenue, with the Athenaeum at the top.

engine Plymouth whistled as it pulled into St. Johnsbury. Ten days later, the first train from Boston pulled into St. Johnsbury. The next issue of the *Caledonian* reported on this happy occasion:

> ## The Cars Have Come!
> *Last Thursday, at about half past four o'clock the first regular train of Passenger Cars came in to town. It was a cheering sight especially for those who have labored so long and diligently to extend the Passumpsic Railroad to this place. There was no formal opening of the Road, but many people were present and a little extemporaneous enthusiasm was exhibited. The arrival was greeted by the ringing of bells, firing of cannon and the cheers of the people assembled upon the station grounds.*

Train service would start with one passenger train and one freight train between St. Johnsbury and Boston daily. The passenger train would involve about ten hours of travel; the freight would cost merchants and manufacturers $1.50 per hundred weights. This would be the start of over one hundred years of rail service with connections to the north, south, east and west.

The Portland and Ogdensburg Railroad opened in December 1875, connecting St. Johnsbury with Portland, Maine. It would be another two years

A train entering St. Johnsbury Center.

before the westward connection was completed. This was seen through by the next generation, led by Erastus's son Horace. This westward connection was a climb from St. Johnsbury to Danville, continuing up to Walden. There were several trestles that had to be built to complete the line; the longest one was the Pumpkin Hill trestle, which was seventy-five feet high and built on a curve. The highest was the one in Walden at ninety-two feet. Many of these trestle areas were eventually filled in. This road was reorganized in 1880 as the St. Johnsbury and Lake Champlain Railroad. At the bottom of one of the stories written about the railroad in St. Johnsbury by Arthur Fairbanks Stone for the *Caledonian-Record* in 1938, this quote appears with no source given, unless by the writer:

> *The St. J. and L.C. Railroad a sinuous pathway wends;*
> *It dips and dives and drops and climbs and twists and curves and bends*
> *'Til through the traveler's dizzied brain this fancy chased and ran*
> *This railroad is constructed on the Zig-Zag plan.*

The railroad depot area consisted of thirteen acres. Located just below the junction of Eastern Avenue and Railroad Street, it held a number of buildings: a passenger station, freight, repair shops, wood house, car house and a semicircular engine house with space for many engines. A new depot was designed by Mr. R.C. Glancy of Boston in 1883. The new 39- by 116-

Engine roundhouse.

The railroad station.

foot depot was constructed of brick and followed the Queen Anne style. Its interior had a waiting room, telegraph and ticket office, dining room, baggage room, two toilets and a small smoking room.

At the time of this writing, there is only the daily freight service between Newport and White River Junction. The State of Vermont purchased the right of way and the Vermont Rail Systems operates the freight service. The depot building was given to the town by the Antonio Pomerleau family and now serves as the Welcome Center and town offices for St. Johnsbury.

## Railroad Street and Depot

At the corner of Eastern Avenue and Railroad Street stood the Passumpsic House, built by Russell Hallett and opened in 1850. Visitors could choose between the St. Johnsbury House and the Passumpsic House for accommodations. Various owners made improvements and had shops rented out as well. O.G. Hale owned the building from 1869 to 1875 and enlarged it to four stories; the building ran 168 feet on Railroad Street and 400 feet on Eastern Avenue. When the ownership changed in 1875, it became known as the Avenue House. In 1896, it was destroyed by fire but immediately rebuilt of brick by Mr. B.G. Howe.

Stores and houses started to appear on Railroad Street. Between 1850 and 1860, shops included lumber being sold north of the Passumpsic House, a shoe shop, a tailor shop, a harness shop, a bakery and Hoyt and Green, which was selling potash and pearl ash.

In the area of the depot were several businesses worth noting. Ephraim Chamberlin opened the first wholesale business just north of the depot in 1850. The business included grain, flour, hardware and oils. Joel Fletcher and his sons ran this business from 1860 to 1878, and then it was run by Griswold and Mackinnon and Pearl. The hardware end had been sold off. In 1892, fire destroyed the building, and Griswold and Mackinnon moved the business to upper Railroad Street. This was a four-story building with an elevator and an annex capable of handling 1,500 tons of grain. The annual business generated approximately $1 million a year. The presence of three large and successful wholesale grain establishments within a half mile of one another (the Mcleod Mills and the Ide Mills were the other two) made St. Johnsbury the leading grain distributing center in this part of the country.

In 1862, the Miller Wagon business moved from Lyndon to St. Johnsbury and for fifty years was successful under the management of Miller and Ryan on Railroad Street. It made carriages, which required multiple skills such

Passumpsic House, corner of Eastern Avenue and Railroad Street. *From* Street, Public Buildings and General Views of St. Johnsbury, Vermont, *published by F.O. Clark.*

as blacksmith, wheelwright, painter and trimmer. A yearly output could be as high as two hundred wheeled vehicles with an additional fifty sleighs. Employing highly skilled workers, the wagon business grew in reputation— "a well known Vermont institution, good for mill or for meeting, for pleasure and for service."

The April 2, 1880 *Caledonian* wrote:

> *The Miller carriages are sold almost everywhere, and orders have been received recently from Minneapolis and Redwood Falls, Minn., where eight were sold at one time, and where they are being sent at intervals. Last year this company built 120 wagons. They build nearly everything that runs on wheels—single and double lumber wagons, express and meat wagons, and all styles of buggies, also hearses.*

A most unique business in 1860 in the depot area to the east was that of a file factory that was run by James Nutt and son Charles, of England. Quoting Edward Fairbanks:

> *The files were subjected to a ten-hour bath in furnaces to draw the temper, then ground to a level surface, in doing which a two-ton grindstone would*

*be used up in a few months; cutting the teeth was a work of extreme nicety and precision, followed by final hardening in crucibles of melted lead and chemical cooling solutions.*

Its largest customer was the E. & T. Fairbanks Company, which in the year 1880 purchased 36,520 files. The factory also re-cut the files for the Howe Scale Company since 1869. Its files were found in machine shops throughout New England and into Canada as well. The Nutt files were all shapes: flat, round or three-cornered, and all sizes: long, short, thin, thick and varying in weight from an ounce to five pounds. The story is told that when Charles Nutt died in 1883, the secret formula died with him and the file factory ended.

The granite monument for the Nutt family in Mount Pleasant can be found by taking the road to the right of the chapel and bearing right at the top of the hill, continuing down the main road and keeping your eyes to the left-hand side. This stone most always provides a giggle from students when they see the name Nutt in large raised letters on the stone. They may have been Nutts all their lives, but they were successful ones.

Also near the depot was the St. Johnsbury Marble Works, started by O.P. Bennett about 1860; before this, Thomas Brigham and Company, followed the next year by Brigham, Spencer and Company, had a marble business. Bennett's supply came from Isle La Motte, Sutherland Falls and West Rutland. He made his own designs, and his work could be found in nearly all the nearby towns. The prices of headstones were from $5 to $100 and monuments ranged from $75 to $500. A writer for the *Caledonian* in 1880 wrote, "We say right here, that to do good work, the stone cutter must have great concentrative power and patience. In this industry one cannot carelessly throw a hammer and chisel, and have them hit the right place at once, but the labor must be slow, persistent, and continuous."

Marble dominated the stonework until the granite quarries in Ryegate, Vermont, opened. In 1867, the St. Johnsbury Granite Company was founded south of the depot by Peter B. Laird. The products were well known and many were statuary in form, some having taken their places in Mount Pleasant Cemetery while others traveled as far as South Carolina. Laird was responsible for the granite foundation and pedestal that the statue *America* stands on honoring the Civil War soldiers. Following the retirement of the Laird brothers, the Carrick brothers continued to operate Granite Square. One order for the Carricks was the Vermont Gettysburg monument, a Corinthian column of thirty-five tons. On top of this column stands a bronze statue of Major General Stannard. The height is sixty-six feet overall.

O.P. Bennett Marble Works, near the depot.

## Newspapers

Without newspapers, it would be hard to tell the history of places, for newspapers are a reflection of the times and ongoing events. One can get a sense of politics, very descriptive reporting of incidents and surely lots of opinions rendered, and not necessarily on an editorial page! St. Johnsbury did have newspapers, beginning with the *Farmer's Herald* in July 1828, a weekly Whig journal edited by Dr. Luther Jewett until 1832. Jewett was born in Canterbury, Connecticut, in 1772, graduated from Dartmouth College in 1792, studied medicine and started practice in St. Johnsbury in 1800. He received ordination as a preacher in 1818 and served as a pastor in Newbury from 1828 to 1832; he was a member of the Vermont Constitutional Convention in 1836, having already served in Congress in 1817, representing the northeast district of Vermont.

The *Farmer's Herald* was printed in a small building where the Academy would be. Dr. Jewett was well suited for being a journalist; his announcement of the paper included these words:

> *The subscriber proposes publishing on St. Johnsbury Plain a newspaper to be called* The Farmer's Herald. *Our free republican institutions can be maintained no longer than intelligence and virtue generally prevail…It will be a prominent object of this paper to furnish such facts as to the character of men and measures that its readers can understandably judge for themselves….Nothing of a religious kind will be admitted which favors one denomination at the expense of another.*

From this newspaper, there were snippets of happenings of early life in St. Johnsbury:

> *Sept. 9, 1828. On Friday, 5th inst. The heavy rains ceased and the work of desolation began. On Sleeper's River the west branch of the Passumpsic, five bridges, one saw mill, one grist mill, one carding machine were swept away. A building occupied by E. and T. Fairbanks was carried off and washed in pieces. Very heavy damage was done to various other works of this ingenious, enterprising and unfortunate company of mechanics, who last winter suffered heavy loss from two fires. Their loss from this fire will be $1000.*

> *June 3, 1829. A most gratifying announcement. Ardent spirit is to be wholly banished from the store of Messrs. Clarks and Bishop on St. Johnsbury Plain. Those who are acquainted with them need not be told that no store in the County is occupied by gentlemen of higher respectability.*

> *Aug. 24, 1831. The Circus saw fit to come parading into our quiet little village on the last Sabbath. Legislative enactments are needed to guard the community against these baleful influences.*

In July 1832, Dr. Jewett turned the newspaper over to Samuel Eaton Jr., who changed the name to the *Weekly Messenger and Connecticut and Passumpsic Valley Advertiser*. It began a decline that resulted in its demise in fifteen months.

In 1837, Albert G. Chadwick came to St. Johnsbury from Concord, New Hampshire, and started the *Caledonian*. This was printed on his hand press in a small building once used for worship at the head of Maple Street. In time, Chadwick built a white cottage on the corner of what is now Winter and Main Streets. Sadly, it was taken down for a parking lot in the 1960s. His tenure of eighteen years as an energetic editor gained him respect and recognition for a fine journal of the times. In 1855, he sold to Rand, Stone and Company, and two years later Charles M. Stone become sole owner. It was said that C.M. Stone was a man of his convictions and did not hesitate to state them, whether they pleased or displeased his readers. He served as editor until his death in 1890, and the paper then passed to his son, Arthur F. Stone. In 1909, the paper was purchased by W.J. Bigelow of Burlington. Herbert Smith took over editorship in 1919. The weekly grew to be a daily, and the *Caledonian-Record* celebrated its 100th birthday on August 9, 1937. It advertised in 1937:

> *Complete Associated Press Wire Service*
> *Associated Press Daily Picture Service*
> *Correspondents in 40 towns of Northeastern Vermont*
> *Associated Press Page of Daily Comics*
> *One of the Best Sports pages in the State*
> *Staff of Six Local News Reporters*
> *Metro Cut Service free to Advertisers*
> *Largest Daily circulation in a town of less than 10,0000 inhabitants in New England*

At this time, the *Caledonian-Record* is being published by the fourth generation of Smiths. Herbert was followed by his son Gordon, who was followed by his son Mark, who is now followed by his son Todd, the current publisher. The paper is a daily with the exception of Sundays.

Another newspaper of note was the *St. Johnsbury Republican*, published for the first time in March 1885. As of 1912, the *Republican* and the *Caledonian* were very similar in content and style. In time, the *Republican* was taken over by the *Caledonian*.

# Thomas Ward

Before we leave Railroad Street, one of the builders of one of the blocks has a rather interesting story. Thomas Ward bought a large lot on the northeast corner of Railroad and Eastern Avenue, where he built the Ward Block in

The Ward Block. *From* Street, Public Buildings and General Views of St. Johnsbury, Vermont, *published by F.O. Clark.*

1870. It was a very large, brick-veneered building that dominated the area until the fire of 1892 destroyed it. While his building skills might receive attention, it was his trial for arson that really sets him apart. The case, *State v. Thomas Ward*, was tried during the December term of 1888. Charges were brought against Ward for setting fire to the barn of Harvey Foster in Walden on the night of January 27, 1886, for motives of revenge. Mr. Ward had been divorced and was then courting a woman who lived with the Fosters. She chose not to keep a relationship with Ward, and the jilted Mr. Ward sought revenge.

His conviction, strangely enough, was solidified by the testimony of a horse. The state was allowed to show that the same horse that Ward had rented from Joseph Clouthier's stable four days before followed the route he had taken with Ward again when driven by Mr. Montgomery. When Montgomery dropped the reins at the turn in the road, the horse went directly to the ruins of the barn. It was pointed out by the state that the Syracuse sleigh used by Ward had wider tracks than others. This sleigh and the horse followed in the same tracks that Ward had made. Ward was found guilty and sent to Windsor State Prison. The Supreme Court upheld the verdict of the lower court. Thomas Ward, convicted by a horse and sleigh, rests in Mount Pleasant Cemetery under the shade of the same spruce that looks down on the Belknaps and Lawrences. The people's stories are as varied as the stones that mark their graves.

# CHAPTER 5

# CROWN JEWELS OF ST. JOHNSBURY

The successful business that the Fairbanks brothers established in this town was only the beginning of the wealth to be given to its townspeople. There were gifts given to the town by Thaddeus, Erastus and Joseph P., followed by their children's gifts that would enrich the town then and for future generations.

## St. Johnsbury Academy

In 1842, St. Johnsbury Academy, often referred to as the Academy, was founded by the three brothers to serve high school–age students. This was at a time when the invention of the platform scale was only twelve years old; the majority of the population of the town was in St. Johnsbury Center, and the Plain still had only one main street running north to south.

The search for a principal for this new school began and ended with James K. Colby from Derry, New Hampshire. Colby had graduated from Dartmouth College in 1838. In the summer of 1842, he accepted the position at St. Johnsbury Academy for $700 a year. He arrived via the stage in early fall and started with an enrollment of twenty-three students. A specific building for the purpose of the Academy had yet to be built, so classes were held in a building known as the Crossman house, located just south of the present-day courthouse. This building owned by the Fairbanks brothers would serve until the fall of 1843, when the first Academy building was completed. Edward T. Fairbanks, oldest son of Joseph P. and Almira, described the building in his *History of St. Johnsbury*: "A graceful structure which introduced a new and classic type amongst the cottages around it. Its low roof of shapely slope, its front adorned with Doric pillars suggested to young eyes a little Greek temple crowning the swell of land with its quiet dignity."

An original Academy building. *Courtesy of Graham Newell.*

The building with the addition of the second story. *Courtesy of Graham Newell.*

This building saw the enrollment jump to 61 members and increase the following year to 164 students. At the close of 1843, the Fairbanks brothers completed legal work that would see the school recognized under Vermont law. This was accomplished by forming a corporation consisting of Thaddeus, Erastus, son Horace, Joseph P. and James K. Colby. The purpose, stated in the organizational agreement, would be "establishing and maintaining a Literary and Scientific Institution located near the South End of the St. Johnsbury Plain." A deed transferred the land and building to this corporation in December 1843.

With the exception of a brief (1856–58) employment in a private school in Philadelphia, James K. Colby served as principal from 1842 until his death in 1866. He was fifty-four when he died of typhoid fever. He saw the enrollment go from twenty-three to two-hundred-plus students. He started teaching in a small building and saw another story added to the first Academy building in 1860 to accommodate the rising enrollment. Lemuel Hastings, in his segment of the book *An Historical Sketch of St. Johnsbury Academy 1842–1922*, wrote of the respect for Colby by his classmates of Dartmouth: "His maturity of mind and character, his stability, his friendliness, as well as his intellectual ability and substantial scholarship had won the respect and admiration of his classmates."

He not only served the Academy well but the town and the South Congregational Church as well. There is a memorial window to James and his wife Sarah Pierce in the church. His character as a Christian, scholar and gentleman certainly fulfilled the Fairbanks brothers' criteria for someone to lead their idea of the Academy forward.

Mount Pleasant Cemetery bears testimony to the memory of James K. Colby. Walking straight out from the chapel, on your left, after a gentle rise in elevation of the road, is a tall granite shaft erected to his memory by the trustees and alumni of the Academy at a cost of $550.

The E. & T. Fairbanks Company met all of the expenses for the Academy for the first twenty-five years. This included buildings, real estate, equipment and debts. After the first twenty-five years, in 1867, Thaddeus Fairbanks assumed financial responsibility for the school. Thaddeus at this time was the last of the founders still living. The year 1873 saw the addition of two new brick buildings by Thaddeus, one known as North Hall and the other South Hall. South Hall was a four-story, forty-five-room dormitory that occupied the space where Colby Hall now stands. South Hall would be destroyed by fire in January 1926. North Hall was destroyed by fire in 1956, having stood where the present Ranger Hall stands now. That fire revealed the encased walls of the original Academy. Thaddeus, besides providing financial support until his death in 1886, also established an endowment of $100,000. Of this total amount, $50,000 came from his brother Erastus's estate, with additional monies supplied by Thaddeus.

A catalogue for St. Johnsbury Academy 1917–18 describes the location of the school this way:

North Hall and South Hall. *Courtesy of William Pearl.*

*Situated at the junction of the Boston and Maine (Passumpsic Division), the St. Johnsbury and Lake Champlain and Main Central Railroads, affording easy and direct means of approach from Portland, Boston, New York, Burlington, and intermediate places. It is an ideal place for a school. The scenery of the region is beautiful and hardly surpassed in New England. The climate is healthful.*

In June 1874, St. Johnsbury's Summer Street high school was closed, sending the twenty-seven students to the Academy. It was determined by District #1 that the cost would be lower to send the students to the Academy rather than maintaining its own high school. Thaddeus, Erastus and Joseph P. would be cheered by the growth of their dream today. Student enrollment is approximately one thousand, and the campus has expanded, taking in the entire south end of the Plain. Descendants of the founders can still be found on the Board of Trustees.

Brantview, home of William P. and Rebecca Fairbanks.

Some of the existing buildings on the Academy's campus have ties to the founding fathers and are worth mentioning before leaving this institution. In 1904, Lady Lucy Webber McMillian donated what had been a privately owned boardinghouse for students attending the Academy. Lady Lucy, the granddaughter of Thaddeus and Lucy Barker Fairbanks, gave the house in memory of her mother, Charlotte Fairbanks Webber. Known as the Charlotte Fairbanks Cottage, it was first used by the Academy as a girls' dormitory. In 1986, it became the home for the business and admissions offices as well as the Twombly Art Center.

In October 1931, Colonel Joseph Fairbanks, grandson of Joseph P., gave Brantview and its thirty acres to the Academy in memory of his mother, Rebecca Pike Fairbanks. Much of the land had been the site of the homestead farm of Joseph P., including fields now used by the athletic department. Brantview (High View) was built in 1884 for William P. Fairbanks (Colonel Joseph's father) and designed by Lambert Packard, a local architect employed by the Fairbanks Company. It is a Queen Anne–style chateau and features a sixty-foot center hall with a grand staircase and beautiful woodwork. The mansion and the carriage house both serve as dormitories today.

William's brother, Edward Fairbanks, had Sheepcote built in 1875 and resided there until his death in 1919. He was the minister of the South Congregational Church and trustee of the Academy for fifty-two years.

In 1976, the Academy purchased Sheepcote, and it too now serves as a dormitory. It should be noted that Edward wrote a *History of St. Johnsbury* through 1912.

Chapter 3 mentions the location of many of the Fairbankses' burial lots. In the same area of the first and second generations of Fairbanks can be found some of the third generation, including Edward, his wife Emma Taplin and their only child, Cornelia. In searching for Edward's brother, William P., the only reference will be on Rebecca Pike Fairbanks's stone: "wife of William P. Fairbanks." William rests in the Woodlawn Cemetery in the Bronx, New York. He and Rebecca parted company and William ended up in Mount Vernon, New York, working for the Fairbanks Company in New York.

# St. Johnsbury Athenaeum

For another "jewel" in the crown of St. Johnsbury, we turn to Horace Fairbanks. Horace was born in 1820, the son of Erastus and Lois Crossman Fairbanks. He entered the family business in 1843 as a clerk; his responsibilities grew until he became head of the company in 1864, at the time of his father's death. He remained at the head of the company until his own passing in 1888 in New York City. Like his father Erastus, he too was elected governor of the state of Vermont, in 1876. While riding across the state on business, he received a telegram: "You are to be Governor of Vermont in spite of yourself." The reasoning behind the wording was that he had declined to be a candidate and refused to have his name entered. The nominating convention at Montpelier found itself unable to agree on any of the three candidates, so Horace's name was introduced without a dissenting vote.

In 1852, Horace Carpenter built the home of Horace and Mary Fairbanks on Western Avenue. This was known as Pinehurst and was located where the old tannery had been. The grounds consisted of three greenhouses, three fish ponds and a deer park that extended up onto Summer Street. A carriage house provided shelter for the various carriages that were used. Pinehurst has survived, first going from the Horace Fairbanks home to become the Maple Grove Tea Room, then to St. Johnsbury Academy and finally to the Elks Club.

On November 27, 1871, the Athenaeum was opened and presented to the town of St. Johnsbury. John Davis Hatch III, an architect from New York, designed the building. Construction had taken three years and was under the direction of Lambert Packard, an architect and chief builder at the scale works.

Pinehurst, home of the Horace Fairbanks family.

The Athenaeum. *Courtesy of William Pearl.*

Horace's goal was to create an extensive library of twelve thousand volumes covering every area of study. To this end, he chose William F. Poole, one of America's most celebrated librarians, to assemble the collection. Poole had been at the Boston Athenaeum for over ten years when approached by Horace. Nothing was spared in assembling this collection; the finest editions of the books were purchased, including those with leather bindings from London. The Athenaeum was intended to be an outstanding library in the town and rivaling most others in the country. Preceding the opening to the public on November 27, the lecture hall was filled on three successive evenings for lectures on the importance of books; these lectures also highlighted the importance of this public lecture hall. In the years to come, the Athenaeum would be visited by two presidents—Benjamin Harrison in 1891 and William Howard Taft in 1912.

A children's room was added in 1924, supporting Horace's belief that the future of the town was in its children. He had shown this in his original collection of books and artworks. Of interest in the children's room are the murals by local artist Margery Eva Lang Hamilton that illustrate classic children's stories.

Nine months after the opening, Hatch was designing an addition to house a permanent art gallery behind the original building; this was completed by 1873. The art gallery is compact and was designed with natural light available through a large central skylight and three smaller skylights high above the north, south and east alcoves. *St. Johnsbury Athenaeum Handbook of the Art Collection* by Mark D. Mitchell reports, "The Athenaeum's art collection may be organized comfortably under several general rubrics: the American landscape, depictions of everyday American life, classical studies, cultural exoticism and reproductions of Renaissance and Baroque masterworks."

There are approximately 120 works that make up the collection today. Horace donated about half of those personally. Many of the remaining number were donated by the granddaughter of Horace, Theodora Willard Best. She had inherited many of the works from her grandfather's estate and donated them shortly after 1900. The gallery and its contents have preserved the time period in which they were given.

The centerpiece of the gallery is Albert Bierstadt's *Domes of the Yosemite*, 1867. This is an oil on canvas and dwarfs you with its size of 116 by 180 inches. When you view it in the gallery, it seems like it was made to be there, but it was originally commissioned for Legrand Lockwood, a financier living in Connecticut. His financial situation was hit hard by the depreciation of gold in 1869, and he was devastated. Lockwood died in 1872, and the painting was sold at auction for $5,100. Lockwood had paid $25,000 when Bierstadt was commissioned to do the work! Purchased now by Horace Fairbanks, the *Domes of the Yosemite* made its way to St. Johnsbury. In the February 1891 issue of *New England Magazine*, Edwin A. Start, in his story called "A Model New England Village," begins by quoting a certain New York newspaper: "And so Bierstadt's magnificent 'Domes' is doomed to the obscurity of a little town in northern Vermont." In his article, Start justifies that indeed the *Domes* is appreciated and deserves its place in the small gallery. It is well worth the trip to see this magnificent building and all that it holds.

The name Athenaeum is appropriate, for it is not just a books and periodicals collection, but it also serves as a reading room, art gallery and lecture hall. In 1996, the Athenaeum was designated a National Historic Landmark by the U.S. Department of the Interior.

Economics of cost and maintenance over the years saw ceilings lowered, doors replaced and other cost-cutting measures taken; fortunately, original pieces were not discarded but stored. In 1996, with the publishing of a Historic Structure Report by Mesick Cohen Wilson Baker Architects of Albany, New York, the Athenaeum began a historic renovation project that allowed for the restoration of the building's original appearance yet modernized its access and use of spaces. This outcome was a tribute to staff and builders, as they achieved a "win-win" accomplishment.

## Fairbanks Museum

The Fairbanks Museum is another of the "crown jewels" of St. Johnsbury. This was a gift to the town by Franklin Fairbanks. Franklin was one of nine children born to Erastus and Lois Crossman Fairbanks, on June 28, 1828, the younger brother of Horace. Franklin was curious of the natural world, whether a rock, plant, bird or animal, and it was that curiosity that started him collecting and would in time provide the nucleus for the museum. At the time of the dedication of the museum in 1891, he held in his hand a grouping of crystals he found on the Willey Slide in the Notch (New Hampshire) at the age of twelve.

He graduated from the Academy at the age of seventeen and entered the Fairbanks scale works. Like his Uncle Thaddeus, he probably knew more of the whole operation than most. He labored in all departments, becoming familiar with "the start to the finish" of the manufacture of the scales. He was mechanical in his own right, making various improvements on scales through the years. In 1856, he was admitted as a partner and succeeded his brother in 1888 to head the company. He would be the last Fairbanks to do so.

Underclyffe mansion, home of Frances and Franklin Fairbanks.

What began as a boyhood collection grew greater as an adult. Lambert Packard designed Underclyffe, which stood on a hill overlooking the Plain and where Franklin's museum would be built. It was a fine example of the Victorian time, with rooms filled with statuary, paintings and large furnishings. By the time Underclyffe was finished in 1872, Franklin had an area approximately thirty-two by forty feet on the third floor housing his "Cabinet of Curiosities." Included in this collection were approximately 450 birds, various rocks and minerals of all shapes and sizes and artifacts from countries such as Egypt, Japan and India. This collection was shared, as it was open to the public on many a Sunday afternoon.

In 1852, he wed Frances A. Clapp, who must have shared his interests, as she allowed this collection on the third floor and some specimens were decorative throughout the mansion as well. As his collection grew, he consulted with architect Lambert Packard as to how his home could be open to the public for the sharing of the collection. This proved to be impractical,

Fairbanks Museum.

so Packard designed the museum. At the dedication on December 15, 1891, Franklin gave tribute to his wife:

> *I cannot let this opportunity pass without grateful mention of the very valuable aid rendered and advise given, by her who is the sharer of my joys and sorrows, the companion of my home. For years we have worked together in making this collection and in planning for this building and to her I feel that much of its success is due.*

It should be noted that when the building was dedicated, it went to the smaller of the two towers and stopped, forming an L-shaped building. In a short time, the building required more space to house its increasing collections, and by March 1895, the addition was completed. This was done by Franklin increasing the space 28½ feet southward and forming a U-shaped building. Franklin was too ill to attend the opening of the addition.

The building is a fine example of Richardson Romanesque style, designed by none other than Lambert Packard. It is built of red sandstone and its outsides should be observed as well as the inside. The faces of Audubon, Agassiz and Humboldt stare southward from the arches of the loggia. These men left their marks on the world of natural history. Other faces stare back at you, and a wonderful limestone frieze sculpture faces Main Street. The entrance is guarded by two bronze lions created by Signor O. Andreoni in

Rome. They are different, and for a reason. The one to the north is a bit forbidding, with its mouthful of teeth and stance of waiting to pounce. This lion was the first to be finished, and when looked at by Franklin and his young daughter Ellen in the studio, Ellen thought the lion to be all right but maybe the next might be a little friendlier. The next one was missing teeth and very relaxed in its position.

The oak, barrel vault ceiling running the full length of the museum is an architectural marvel. The main floor for the most part displays the wonders of the natural world, from bear to bat, polar bear to passenger pigeon, moose to mouse. One feature on the main floor is the created dioramas of the Lunenburg, Vermont taxidermist William Balch. He was one of the first to create lifelike dioramas showing not only his skill as a taxidermist but also that of an artist and naturalist. Note should be made that they were created without the availability of styrofoam, plastic and aluminum.

The balcony area is a potpourri of the wide variety of collections given the museum. They range from Japanese netsuke to fossils, from Egyptian mummies to objects from the Civil War. Franklin encouraged those who traveled to bring things back to the museum, and the balcony reflects this.

The museum grew with the installation of the only public planetarium in Vermont and the Northern New England Weather Center, where weather broadcasts emanate daily to local radio stations and Vermont Public Radio's "Eye on the Sky."

One other note about Franklin and his collection: his desire was for more than a building to house his collection; he wanted people to learn from it. A classroom was designated for this purpose in the original blueprints. In this respect, he was a true pioneer in his desire that students should learn. His words were, "But let me say here that a collection of birds, animals, shells or whatever it may be, is after all but a collection of dead things, unless used as an illustration to help in your search for knowledge." His vision lives on with two classrooms and thousands of schoolchildren being taught yearly using the collections.

Underclyffe, however, did not survive as the second generation lost its money and the family was forced to sell. The buyers were more interested in the real estate and multiple houses, and therefore the mansion deteriorated to the point of no return and was torn down in 1938.

This chapter has highlighted three of the gifts left to the town of St. Johnsbury by the Fairbanks family but is by no means all that they did. There were the churches that they helped to build and sustain; the YMCA building given by Henry Fairbanks (son of Thaddeus and Lucy) in 1885. As to what sum of money was given to the "good of the town," no one will ever know, but the three "jewels" described certainly make St. Johnsbury a destination today.

The interior of the Fairbanks Museum.

Horace and Franklin are again found in Mount Pleasant Cemetery by the middle road, keeping the tall spruce as your destination. Keep the spruce to your left and you will continue straight and walk right into Franklin's final resting place, shaded by a large Norway spruce. One complaint can be found with Franklin and Frances's monument—her maiden name is not given. The name was Clapp, and if you turn 180 degrees and look to your left for the spire, you will be looking at her parents. Frances's father, Sumner, was the first minister of the South Congregational Church. If you then let your eyes turn right on that same terrace and follow to the end, you will find Horace and family. There is a granite wall around their plot with the name "Horace Fairbanks" printed on the steps leading to the plot. Facing Franklin's monument again, look to the left on the first terrace across the road; a small upright stone with "Mary P. Smith" can be found, with her death listed as taking place at Underclyffe. Curiosity about this statement led to the revelation that she was their cook. The stone also reveals that she came from Ireland. If only stones could talk!

# CHAPTER 6

# BUSINESSES

## Moose River Works—Ely Fork and Hoe

Summerville was located across the Passumpsic River, where there was no bridge in the early days except by going around to Paddocks Village. A bridge spanned what became known as the Portland Street about 1856, leading directly to the Summerville area. Summerville was its own separate village until 1890, when it was annexed to the village of St. Johnsbury. James Harris came from Kirby and bought the hill (area to the left of the present Memorial Bridge) that bore his name—Harris Hill—from where a great many pictures were taken over the years. Summerville had a successful business on the Moose River. The Moose River Works was started by George W. Ely in 1848, and for sixty-six years it manufactured hoes and forks of the highest quality. The business was perfected over the years in a new process of forging that made it possible to turn out one thousand tools daily. The forks were known for their durability and shapeliness, as found in the newspaper the *Daily Herald*:

> *In Agricultural Hall we saw the exhibitor of the Ely forks stick the tines into a board and literally twist them one over the other like string, as soon as released they would fly back to the original position…Hoes were tested in the same way, sticking the blade into a board and bending it back almost to a semi-circle but without the least injury. These are without exception the best articles of the kind we have ever seen; they are the constant wonder and admiration of the crowds who gather to see them tested.*

Fires in 1859 and 1895 destroyed the factory but resulted in better buildings almost immediately. In 1902, the American Fork and Hoe Company took over with offices at Cleveland, Ohio. Up until just a few years ago, it was

Miles Hovey, a cooper. *Courtesy of Fairbanks Museum.*

manufacturing just handles for agricultural tools. At the time of this writing, the site and buildings sit empty and the area is one of several being considered for a new fire station.

There were three other smaller business ventures in Summerville. Miles Hovey was known for his excellent water tubs on the street in the horse and buggy days. The story is told of one Halloween long ago when some mischievous souls replaced the *C* of "Cooper" with a *P*! Napoleon Flint and Ezra P. Magoon had a shoe peg factory near Arthur Smith's store in 1864. For some time, their daily output was sixty bushels of wooden pegs. In 1895, Captain E.L. Hovey was bottling sulphur water from Asisqua spring off the avenue of the same name on the Moose River.

## Ide Mills—E.T. & H.K. Ide Company

In 1879, St. Johnsbury became the headquarters for the E.T. & H.K. Ide mills. The Ides' venture into milling was started in 1813 by Timothy Ide, who bought a gristmill in Passumpsic, Vermont. The St. Johnsbury location was about three acres on Bay Street that lay between Portland Street and Eastern Avenue. The land was partially swampy but reclaimed and provided enough ground for new buildings. After the mill burned at Passumpsic and a new one purchased at Lyndon Falls met the same fate, a new mill was constructed on Bay Street in 1905. A circular corn bin with a twelve-thousand-bushel capacity was also part of the building project. The elevator building erected before stood fifty feet high, with four floors of fifty by eighty feet. Adjoining this was a coal plant with bins into which fifteen hundred tons of coal could be dumped from the railroad cars. There was enough equipment in the mill to make it possible to grind three thousand bushels of grain a day and store thirty thousand bushels of bulk grain. Add to this the capacity of one thousand tons of sacked flour and feed and you had a major operation. William Adams Ide was the fourth generation to head up the Ide business, and he had an interesting quote about the miller:

> The miller likes his work and takes pride in it. He likes the sight and feel of good grain. He can tell at a glance the quality, and if there is one kernel of damaged corn or one wild oat in a sample, he will detect it instantly. He likes the noise of the mill and his ear is attuned to it, so that he instantly notices any change in the speed. He even likes the fine white dust from the grinding. It smells good and it tastes good and gives his lungs something to work on.

The E.T. & H.K. Ide Company was being managed by the sixth generation when it sold its last store and the company closed its doors in 2001.

## St. Johnsbury Bakery—Cross Bakery

John S. Carr started the St. Johnsbury Bakery on Main Street where St. John's Church stands today. Over the next approximately fifteen years, it was owned and operated by Winter, Willey & Co., Carr & Joy, W.P. Fairbanks and finally sold to George Cross. George's father had been in the business in Montpelier and developed the cracker. The bakery in St. Johnsbury was known for its crackers, and in the *Caledonian* of 1880 some of the inner workings of the bakery were described. The bakery was producing 30 barrels of crackers per day. Flour came from Minneapolis, from 1,800 to 2,000 barrels yearly. Thirty thousand pounds of the "best refined lard" came from Chicago by the railcar load. The bakery employed ten to fourteen men who were paid weekly.

The dough was mixed by steam-powered machinery. The next morning, the dough was put through rollers, making it into sheets the right thickness, and then through the cutting machine, which sliced the dough into cracker size, whereupon it was taken by a "shovel" and put into the oven. Picture this—the oven had a large rotary, horizontal disc made out of soapstone. The disc was sixteen feet, six inches in diameter and was evenly heated by coal. Coal amounts of sixty to seventy tons a year were used by the bakery. This oven had the capacity of baking two barrels of crackers at a time; a barrel held 1,100 to 1,200 crackers. The barrels were lined with paper to prevent the crackers from absorbing any "odors or substance." There were several different kinds of crackers made, including common, oyster, soda, graham and picnic ones. The crackers were the main part of the business but the company did bake other things such as buns, rolls, cookies, cake and bread.

In the 1890s, George had to move his bakery to Railroad Street because his need to expand on Main Street had met with opposition. This three-story brick building once stood where Uniquity store is located, right next to Caplans Army Store. George H. Cross retired in 1911, and the business was bought by Wilbur Davis and Benjamin Scribner, who did business under the name George H. Cross, Inc. In 1927, Montpelier and St. Johnsbury bakeries became C.H. and George H. Cross, Inc.; crackers were then made in Montpelier and bread in St. Johnsbury. Approximately fifty thousand loaves were made weekly in 1937. The business was bought and moved to

Cross Bakery on Railroad Street. *Courtesy of Fairbanks Museum.*

Claremont, New Hampshire, in 1965. The common crackers were often described as dry, bland or neutral; most people just liked them! Many an older reader will remember a relative having crackers and milk for Sunday night supper—that is, breaking the crackers up in a bowl and pouring milk over them. The recipe for the crackers lives on, for the Vermont Country Store bought the recipe in 1981 and was making them in Rockingham, Vermont. They are sold under the name of Vermont Crackers in stores all over. The cracker has shrunk a bit and now comes in plastic bags.

# The Courthouse

Caledonia County was organized in 1786 and Danville became the shire town, a position that it held for sixty years. Danville held the county seat without opposition until 1838. In October of that legislative session, a petition was presented from Sheffield, Burke, St. Johnsbury, Kirby, Barnet, Sutton, Waterford, Newark and Wheelock to change the location, claiming the rough, hilly roads made it difficult to get there. This first removal attempt was defeated, as was the second, but the third time was the charm to change the location—but not necessarily to St. Johnsbury. Hearings were held to determine the location, which would be somewhere on the Passumpsic between Steven's Village in Barnet and Lyndon Centre. At the close of the hearings, St. Johnsbury was chosen as the shire town. Reporters from the *Caledonian* of St. Johnsbury and the *North Star* of Danville left no doubt that this was a decision that involved a great deal of emotion. This continued even while construction was going on.

The site chosen for the courthouse was where the old burial ground was on the Plain. According to Edward Fairbanks, "Meantime as a place for burial this enclosure had become wholly inadequate: as a town charge it had suffered the neglect that commonly befell such enclosures; its tangles of briar roses and other decorative miscellany running wild could not make it an ornamental feature on the main street."

With the opening of Mount Pleasant Cemetery, many had already had their loved ones moved. Others were encouraged to do so as proper license had been obtained, under which friends of persons buried there could remove them. If they wanted the Cemetery Association to do so, it would be at a cost not to exceed two to three dollars each, according to the *Caledonian* of October 14, 1854.

William C. Arnold, representing the Jonathan Arnold heirs, made a quit-claim deed releasing all claims to the land originally given by Jonathan for

The courthouse. *From* Street, Public Buildings and General Views of St. Johnsbury, Vermont, *published by F.O. Clark.*

the use of a burial ground, school or any other public building. This being accomplished, a $13,000 contract for the building was awarded to E. & T. Fairbanks & Company.

The courthouse building was designed by J.D. Tonle. It would also house a new town hall. Because of this combination, the town and county shared the costs of construction and future maintenance. The town of St. Johnsbury would pay approximately one-fourth of each. Tonle's plans called for a brick building with brown stone trimmings in the Italianate style, fronting ninety-six feet on Main Street. The courtroom was to be fifty-two by fifty-seven feet and a town hall fifty-two by sixty-five feet, along with offices and space for vaults holding records. The building was started in May 1856 and completed in time to seat the December term court of 1856. In the spring of 1857, grading and the planting of elm trees took place. Thirty-three years later, improvements were made to the interior, an annex on the east side and a spacious vault installed for records and documents.

From 1994 to 2000, University of Vermont archaeology students carefully dug and sifted through the area that was going to be disturbed for a courthouse expansion. This project confirmed that the first exhumations done in the 1850s had not been complete. All remains were reburied in Mount Pleasant Cemetery with a headstone that reads:

*Early Settlers*
*Of St. Johnsbury*
*Left behind 1852–1856*
*During*
*Caledonia Courthouse*
*Construction*
*Rediscovered 1994–2000*
*During*
*Courthouse Expansion*

*REUNITED WITH*
*FRIENDS AND FAMILY*

The courthouse expansion monument to bodies left behind in the old burying ground.

# St. Johnsbury Trucking

The Zabarsky brothers grew up in Orleans County. By 1920, Harry was driving a truck, collecting milk from farms and hauling it to a creamery in Barton. The truck hauling had a limited "season" from May to November before teams of horses had to haul the milk because of the road conditions. He later came to St. Johnsbury and started doing general trucking; he picked up delivery of meat for Swift and Co. when he was only twenty years of age. He was then joined by his younger brother Mickey, and by 1925, St. Johnsbury Trucking was well established and advertising in the *Caledonian-Record* for general trucking. The roads were still mostly dirt, and icy conditions found more trucks in ditches than not. Covered bridges proved problematic too—Mickey and a helper went through the one at Lyndon Corners with a load of lumber. Right after the 1927 flood, they were hired by the postmaster to deliver mail to Newport. The first trip of forty-six miles took twenty-six hours. Open trucks led to closed, insulated bodies, with the first box being recovered from a dump in Medford, Massachusetts, and put on a Brockway truck. A big test came during the Depression. The trucking industry was a bit chaotic, and in 1935, legislation put it under the jurisdiction of the Interstate Commerce Commission. The company was hit with a bit of a bookkeeping issue and found itself $90,000 in debt. On it went, and within three years the creditors were paid off. Fast forward to 1964, when the corporation (formed in 1932) listed 1,010 units, including trucks, trailers and tractors and more on order.

Maurice had also joined the business, and the three brothers saw roads go from dirt to interstates, trailers from eighteen feet to forty and weight limitations from forty to seventy-three thousand pounds. The company had a large terminal on Portland Street where the White Market is today. In 1953, the trucking company acquired office space on Main Street where the old brick Fairbanks store had been. In February 1954, it held an open house in this office space. At this time, the trucking company had over eight hundred employees and twenty-one company-owned terminals. Many a homesick person was cheered when he saw the familiar St. Johnsbury truck traveling down the road. According to the *New York Times* of 1993, St. Johnsbury Trucking Company was "A Victim of the Deregulated Road." The industry was deregulated in 1980; by that time, all but nine of the top fifty trucking companies operating in 1978 had closed or merged. The company had restructured its finances twice since 1991 to lighten the debt load that it incurred in 1986 from a leveraged buyout.

# Cary Maple Sugar Company and Maple Grove

The story begins at the Gray farmhouse just three miles south of St. Johnsbury in 1915. Helen was a student of home economics at Columbia University and was home for the summer. She wanted to experiment with maple sugar in the hopes of making good candy. She asked her good friend, Ethel McLaren, to join her and the two joined forces with the blessing of Katherine Ide Gray, Helen's mother. They worked all summer with pleasing results. By experimenting, they made their own recipe, and word got out. The first customer was Mrs. Henry Fairbanks, who received the first box. Success was theirs, and a back shed was converted into a candy kitchen. But demand exceeded space, so in 1920 Horace Fairbanks's mansion, Pinehurst, was bought and they moved the operation to Western Avenue. This was a major undertaking and other means had to be found in order to meet the overhead costs. The Maple Grove Tea Room came first, followed by the Maple Grove Inn.

In time, in addition to the maple bonbons, they produced over seventy different kinds of chocolates and manufactured maple sugar, maple cream and maple syrup in many different ways. They expanded into New York and opened a restaurant and salesroom under the name Maple Grove Products.

Helen Gray packaging candies.

Cary Maple Sugar Company.

Maple Grove Candies, Inc., was formed in 1920 by George Cary; Helen, Ethel, Katherine and Gertrude Franklin; and three ladies who made Mary Elizabeth candies in New York. The year 1929 saw Maple Grove Candies, Inc., bought by George Cary and Earl Franklin. A manufacturing plant was proposed and started at the end of Portland Street, just inside the village limits.

George Cary was already in the maple business, quite by accident. He was a drummer for a wholesale grocer in Maine and traveled a great deal in Vermont. He found a customer that wanted to pay his order with 1,500 pounds of maple sugar. He accepted the offer and then found that his firm did not see things the way he did—he was stuck with the sugar! In his travels, he met a salesman for tobacco; upon questioning how cut plug tobacco was made, he was told that it was dipped in West Indies sugar for taste, which caused it to stick together when pressed. He wondered, "Why West Indies sugar when you can get maple sugar cheaper?" The tobacco salesman was cautious and only took 200 pounds to start, but soon he was back for more. Cary was on his way to becoming the maple sugar king of the country. In 1904, he organized the Cary Maple Sugar Company, which grew by leaps and bounds and established St. Johnsbury as the maple center of the world.

What goes up sometimes comes down hard, and such was the case with George. When he raised the price of sugar, his major customer cut his ties and went to Canada. In 1931, being in poor health, George Cary resigned as president of Cary Maple Sugar Company. Clinton Cary and Earl Franklin left the company, and in September, George gave up and filed for bankruptcy. However, this did not affect Maple Grove. The Cary Company was bought by the Fear Company, a food packinghouse in Brooklyn, New York, in 1952. In 1953, the Maple Grove Company was bought by Harold Whaley, who had been the plant manager for many years. At the present time, it is owned by B&G Foods of Parsippany, New Jersey. It is called Maple Grove Farms of Vermont and resides in the same Portland Street building. It boasts of being the largest manufacturer of maple candies in the world, the largest packer of pure maple syrup in the United States and the best-selling line of specialty dressings in the United States.

## St. Johnsbury Hospital

The beginning of the St. Johnsbury Hospital dates back to 1892 and Reverend J.A. Boissonnault, rector of Notre Dame de Victoire Church. He realized the need "for an asylum for aged, poor and infirm persons, and for children bereft of their parents." He bought the Dr. Perkins property on the Prospect Street site, and in 1894, four Sisters of Charity from Providence, Canada, arrived to visit the poor and the sick in their homes and take in those who needed more care. The first year recorded 1,583 visits made to homes, and four older people and five orphans were given shelter. Within a year, this home proved to be inadequate to meet the needs; it was demolished, and on May 26, 1895, the cornerstone was in place for a new building. The new building was dedicated "to the service of God and humanity" on November 18, 1895. A few days after the opening, the first hospital patient was admitted, reportedly a victim of an accident in the Fairbanks factory.

In the second year, the home and hospital recorded 1,510 visits to homes, two aged people taken in and the number of orphans rose to seventeen. In 1900, it was decided that all care and attention be given to the sick and other institutions would care for the others. In October of that same year, the first trained nurse came to work from Montreal. Electric lights were installed, the operating room was equipped with modern sanitary equipment plus a marble floor and marble lavatories were added for the use of physicians.

An interesting note of 1902 is that Mr. Turner, superintendent of Fairbanks factory, made arrangements to pay the hospital $250 a year for a bed for any poor employee of the company who required hospital care. This arrangement was in effect until 1915.

St. Johnsbury Hospital.

In 1928, there was a major expansion completed, doubling the space (four stories) and adding an elevator and a solarium on each floor. In a *Souvenir Book of St. Johnsbury Hospital* from 1892–1928, it reports that at the end of the thirty-sixth year of the hospital's existence all bills were paid, a grand total of 7,150 patients were treated and 2,843 operations had been performed. The last renovations occurred in 1955, and by the following decade the building was deemed out of date for use as a hospital

## Brightlook Hospital

In January 1899, twenty-three citizens (fourteen were resident physicians) formed an association to found, maintain and operate a hospital in St. Johnsbury. The corporate name was Brightlook. The first Brightlook Hospital was begun in the former home of Erastus Fairbanks on Western Avenue. A favorable lease was agreed upon, alterations made and on June 23, 1899, the dedication of the five-bed hospital was attended by one thousand people. This was to be a short-term fix, for the building was inadequate, the location was not favorable and funds were lacking.

In 1905, with a deficit of $700, a citizens' meeting was held at the museum to find out the people's wishes and form a plan. A woman offered

The first Brightlook Hospital, located in Erastus Fairbanks's home.

a gift of $5,000, with the stipulation that $10,000 more be raised by January 1908. Old Reservoir Hill was purchased for the second Brightlook, and on May 1, 1907, the *Caledonian* reported that workmen had taken down the fifty-year-old reservoir on top of the hill at the foot of Summer Street. The foundation was bedrock and would serve nicely for the building. June 26 saw the breaking of the ground for the expected $25,000 hospital. The plans submitted by architect A.I. Lawrence of Burlington were accepted. On March 14, 1908, the second Brightlook was dedicated. That summer, following the dedication, E.M. Taft donated several hundred dollars worth of work in cutting down the knoll to the north, constructing a winding road and improving the grounds in front of the hospital.

The Hospital Aid Association was organized in July 1899 with 65 women as members. This organization provided much to the hospital in miscellaneous ways, in addition to its monetary giving, which amounted to $7,200 in money and equipment over the first ten years. There was a two-year training school for nurses. The lectures were provided by resident physicians and surgeons at no charge to this department. In 1912, Edward Fairbanks wrote that there were 447 patients treated, 324 of these requiring surgery; 6 nurses were graduated and 14 were still in training.

In 1912, a foundation was laid for a nurses' home just south of the hospital. The building was completed and dedicated on March 14, 1914, at a cost of

The second Brightlook Hospital, with nurses' home to the left.

$33,000. It included central heating and a power plant in the basement. This addition was named the Rebecca P. Fairbanks Home for Nurses, as Rebecca had been the principal donor.

Brightlook Hospital served the community and towns around it until 1972. At the time of its closing, it had served over 150,000 patients and had fifty beds and ten bassinets. The building is now an apartment building and the nurses' home is condominiums.

As for the first Brightlook Hospital, its life ended in 1957, having been built approximately 125 years earlier by Erastus Fairbanks. It served as the "executive mansion" while Erastus was governor (1852 and 1860). It was from his home that he wrote and issued the call for a special session of the legislature when the Civil War began. After his death, it served as the home of his daughter Sarah, who married Charles M. Stone, editor and publisher of the *Caledonian*. At the closing of Brightlook, it became a residential building. In 1948, it was sold to the Ralph J. Mollica Post VFW, which maintained it as a clubroom until it was sold to C.H. Goss Company. Its history is summed up by a caption under a photo of it being razed in the *Caledonian-Record:* "WHERE HOSPITAL WAS BORN AND CIVIL WAR DECLARED."

# Photographers

What would history be like if we could not look at old photographs? Mention must be made of these pioneers. St. Johnsbury's pioneer photographer was F.B. Gage. In 1851, he opened the St. Johnsbury Portrait Gallery in the Emerson Hall Block, where the Athenaeum now stands. Gage was described not only as a photographer but also as an artist, poet and philosopher and "somewhat eccentric." His ads in the *Caledonian* often referred to himself as "The- Man-With-The-Long-Flowing-Beard" or "Old Daguerreen." The ads often included a somewhat whimsical poem:

*For twenty-five cents*
*Is all the expense*
*Of an Ambrotype made of your face*
*And for double that sum*
*If you presently come,*
*'Twill be made and put in a case*

He added landscapes to his trade, and one can occasionally find a stereoscope card that shows his ability as a photographer. He sometimes placed himself in his photographs. One of his highly prized photos was that of Willie Johnson, a fourteen-year-old St. Johnsbury drummer boy of the Civil War who received the Medal of Honor for keeping his drum at the retreat of the Union soldiers at Harrison Landing. In 1866, Gage had his gallery across the street in the Brown Block. W.M. Kellogg, another photographer, also occupied this space. This block is still occupied by photographers—the fourth generation of the Jenks family.

Longtime photographers included T.C. Haynes and C.H. Clark on Eastern Avenue. Another well-known photographer was D.A. Clifford, who practiced over the post office block on Main Street. Clifford served as vice-president of the American Photographers Association until his death in 1889.

# Passumpsic Savings Bank

In October 1852, some men saw the need to establish a mutual savings bank, and they secured a charter from the Vermont legislature. On February 24, 1853, the Passumpsic Savings Bank began business on Main Street. Barron Mouton was the president, with J.P. Bancroft the vice-president. On opening day, seventeen depositors from St. Johnsbury, Danville and Waterford started savings accounts; when the day finished, the bank had received $863. The first customer was Samuel W. Slade, a practicing attorney in town, who made a deposit of $150. The banking hours were from 2:00 to 5:00 p.m. on Thursday afternoons. The first statement was issued on March 17, 1853, by E.C. Redington, treasurer, showing total assets of $3,800.86 and total liabilities of $3,800.86. The total number of depositors was sixty-three—forty-one males and twenty-two females.

The bank operated as a mutual savings bank until April 1996, when it reorganized as a state-chartered stock bank. It is now a stock savings bank and is a wholly owned subsidiary of Passumpsic Bancorp, a mutual holding company. It is the largest independent bank in Vermont's Northeast Kingdom, with branches in St. Johnsbury, Danville, Lyndonville, Newport and Island Pond. It also has a presence in New Hampshire now, with offices in Lancaster, Whitefield, Groveton and Littleton.

# Mount Pleasant Cemetery

Returning to Mount Pleasant Cemetery and visiting some of the folks in this chapter, you start at the chapel, take the road to the right, go to the top of the big hill and turn right. George Cross is found on the left in the front row, just before the area is bisected by a road. It is a large granite monument symbolic of the early 1900s, when stones were quite large and without much symbolism on them. The story is told that when George went to Boston on business and entered the hotel, he was asked if "he might have the same suite of rooms that his son had when he came." George replied, "No, that man has a rich father, I do not."

Continue your journey straight from George to St. Johnbury's mini Washington monument, on the right. It is the Ide monument, consisting of thirty-five tons of granite. The spire alone took sixteen horses to pull it from the depot area to the cemetery. The stone is not obtrusive, sitting in the curve of the road with the trees in the back; one might ponder what kind of foundation is under that massive weight that allows it to stand so straight and true? Katherine Ide Gray is there, along with daughter Helen. E.T. & H.K. Ide markers are in the front. Horace Knight was part of the cavalry in the Civil War. Henry Clay Ide is there with a respectable résumé on his stone: chief justice of Samoa, minister to Spain and governor general of the Philippines. He also served as St. Johnsbury Academy's headmaster for two years following the death of James Colby.

The spire of the Ide monument being pulled by sixteen horses from the railroad depot. *Courtesy of Mount Pleasant Cemetery.*

Continue straight down the road past Mr. Nutt, and as you go through a four-way intersection, keep your eyes peeled for Ely on the left. On the right will be a number of doctors of St. Johnsbury and Brightlook Hospitals, including Farmer, Crampton, Allen and others. This section is often called Doctors' Row by those of us familiar with its residents!

# CHAPTER 7

# HOUSES OF WORSHIP

## First Church

Let us return to that first meetinghouse in the Center, built in 1804 to provide the foundation of religious services in the lives of these early settlers. There were no regularly held Sunday services and no specific denominations. The majority of pew holders were Universalists. The meetinghouse did not have a bell tower or a bell of any kind, nor did it have a chimney. The idea of heat had not been considered at all, and the womenfolk brought their foot warmers, which were replenished from Lieutenant Pierce's fireplace. The pulpit stood ten feet high on the east side with a winding stairway. As time went on, there were a few conditions called for the town to take action on, such as:

- voted that Captain Barney keep the meetinghouse clean and that it be swept at least twice a year
- voted that no person be allowed to enter the pulpit on town meeting days unless directed by the town
- voted that five people be appointed to expel dogs from the meetinghouse on Sundays

On November 21, 1809, 19 men and women did not feel that they could live without the ordinances of the church and agreed on this date to do their part in maintaining them. One of the leading men was Hubbard Lawrence, the tanner, who served as a deacon and moderator. David Stowell, a farmer on Bible Hill, served as a deacon and clerk of this group. It would be six years before a minister could be had for the organization. By the tenth year, the number had risen by 113 members.

Churches of St. Johnsbury.

## Universalist

At the annual meeting of October 1837, it was voted to build a Universalist church at the Center Village. The building was erected at the northwest corner of the Center Village burial ground in 1843. A bell of around one thousand pounds was added a year later; it rang out faithfully until 1876, when the building was destroyed in a fire.

## Second Congregational–North Congregational

The first meetinghouse on the Plain was a small house at the head of the Plain that history records was used as a dwelling, a store, a distillery and a meat market before 1818, when it was moved down to the head of what is Maple Street today. Here it was made over for a temporary house of worship by David Smith. Luther Clark shouldered most of the expenses, which included rows of benches, a platform with a desk at the upper end and a Canadian box stove. This meetinghouse was to have heat! This was called the Second Congregational, having set off from the First Congregational in the Center. This became the meetinghouse for people living on the Plain, who had gone to the Center before. In Edward Taylor Fairbanks's *History of St. Johnsbury*, he sought memories from Mrs. Lydia Jones about the meetinghouse. Among them was the memory of a Mr. Melvin, an elderly, very deaf gentleman who stood by the side of the minister holding his ear trumpet all the time he was speaking. She also recalled her aunt, Mrs. Nat Brown, standing and reaching over the heads of people in front of her to wake Deacon Clark with the point of her umbrella.

This building served as a place of religious meeting for nine years before it became a store again. Following this versatile building, we find its next use as a school. In 1837, it was equipped with a printing press, from which came the first issues of the *Caledonian*. Then it was again a dwelling before it journeyed down the street and served again as a dwelling until 1885, when its life ended as it was torn down to make way for the Passumpsic Savings Bank Block.

In the summer of 1827, a meetinghouse was constructed where the North Church is today. The lot was given by Deacon Luther Clark. The pulpit was between the two entrance doors—one could not sneak into this building late. The pews were high backed with doors. The first minister was James Johnson. This meetinghouse had a bell and an organ. In 1847, this building took a ride down to the edge of the old burying ground, where it was eventually gifted to the Academy in 1856. Buildings sure did move around in the town's early history. From the records of this meetinghouse in 1839 we find the following notice: "The bell ringing for meetings, building of fires, sweeping paths in winter and trimming and filling of lamps in the meeting house for one year, was bid off at fourteen dollars."

## Mormons

About this particular point in time, another religion was being introduced by Joseph Smith of Sharon, Vermont, who came to the Chesterfield Hollow (north of East St. Johnsbury) in 1835. Joseph had started his new religion in 1830. In 1835, he arrived with some of his followers and caused quite a stir. Headquartered in Chesterfield Hollow, meetings were held in one of the Snow family farm barns. One of Smith's claims was the power to cure the sick by the laying on of hands. Many were converted and baptized in the stream that ran near the barn. This excitement caused a number of families, including the Snows, to sell their land and follow Smith to "the promised land," which at that time was Kirtland, Ohio. One woman who witnessed the leaving of the large canvas-covered wagons and families said, "I remember seeing them start off, and one woman stopped as they passed the East Village grave-yard, and went in to visit her child's grave before they left the place forever."

In 1849, Erastus Fairbanks Snow, born here in 1818, was ordained one of the twelve apostles of the Latter Day Saints and served for forty years. Some thought his preaching ability was better than that of Brigham Young, in the southern states. Snow converted hundreds. William Snow, born here in 1806, was one of the first two Mormon pioneers to get to Salt Lake Valley, where he too became an apostle.

## Second Congregational

Returning to the Congregational Church, a second building was erected on the same location in 1847 to house the growing congregation. It was built in the Christopher Wren style of architecture, much like the present-day South Congregational Church. The church faced Main Street, as did the pulpit. The building had a vestry where meetings could be held and Sunday school classes taught. The cost for this new building was $7,000.

Meanwhile, East Village was thriving with its grist-, saw- and carding mills and its starch and oatmeal factories. Its residents also desired a church, so

Second Congregational Church, as seen from the courthouse looking north.

they built the present-day meetinghouse. The Third Congregational Church was organized and dedicated on November 25, 1840.

## South Congregational

With the railroad opening in 1850, there was an increase in population and an increase in church attendance, which resulted in yet another space constraint that had to be dealt with. The issue was discussed long and emotionally with the conclusion that the present church must be divided in two. Sixty-five members were set off to make up the new church; on October 23, 1851, they were organized under the name South Congregational Church. Any older

South Congregational Church. *From* Street, Public Buildings and General Views of St. Johnsbury, Vermont, *published by F.O. Clark.*

members of the congregation that was split off had the option of declining if the move was to be too painful. Even though it was the only thing that seemed doable, it was emotional. The Reverend Sumner Clapp was the first minister of the South Church. This church was dedicated on January 14, 1852. South is the only present-day example of the Wren architecture in St. Johnsbury. With the naming of the new church the South Congregational, it seemed only fitting to have the Second Congregational Church called the North Congregational Church.

## North Congregational

For the first ten years after the South Congregational was built, the predictions of increased population did not materialize. The churches struggled, and there was even talk of reunion. However, the next ten years saw the church population increase to the point where more room was needed. In 1875,

North Congregational Church with the church manse.

the State Young Men's Christian Association was canvassing the state of Vermont. Turnout was huge at the meetings, and space was once more addressed at the North Church. In early February 1877, there was talk of building a third building. Franklin and Horace Fairbanks solved the problem of what to do with the present building; they had bought the corner lot where the present-day Colonial Apartment building now stands, and they offered the lot rent-free for the present church to move there. Moved on rollers, it was later converted into the music hall. The new building, designed by Lambert Packard, was of Isle La Motte stone; its style is that of Medieval Gothic, with an interior of native cherry wood. The organ was given by Charles Fairbanks (brother to Franklin and Horace) and consisted of 1,789 pipes! The length of the building is 162 feet and the top of the turret above the bell tower is 140 feet. One bit of irony is that at the base of the tower forming the foundation are stones from the county jail in Danville. The seating capacity was eight hundred; presently it is nearer to seven hundred, with some seats having been removed. The true cost has never been revealed because Horace and Franklin took the contract at the already raised $37,000.

# Methodists

The Methodist church was organized in St. Johnsbury in 1856. Services were held in the old Union Hall at the corner of Main and Central Streets until January 1859, when a church building was completed on Central Street. In 1880, the parsonage was built next door at a cost of $2,700. By this time, the membership was bursting at the seams, and the building was enlarged and dedicated on January 31, 1884, complete with modern appliances. In 1908, it was damaged by fire but was remodeled. On January 14, 1915, fire again took the building beyond repair. The name Grace Methodist Church was adopted in 1892. The present Vermont granite structure was constructed and dedicated in 1916. A wonderful feature is its Tiffany of New York stained-glass window, dedicated to the memory of Hiram N. Turner and given by his wife Ellen. The Gothic window of five openings represents "The Annunciation to the Shepherds." It measures twelve by twenty feet. A tradition over the years has been that on the Sunday before Christmas, the congregation stands and faces the window in the singing of "O Little Town of Bethlehem."

The Center Village's third church was of the Methodist denomination in 1841. Prior to the building of the church, a small house had served as a house of worship. For about eighty years, regular services were held by the

Grace Methodist Church.

The former Methodist Church, which became Green Mountain Grange #1 in Center.

Methodists. After the turn of the century, with better travel, it got harder to support the church. It was turned over to the Green Mountain Grange #1, the first Grange order in New England, to be used as a community hall and lodge room.

East St. Johnsbury had a Methodist presence as well beginning in 1840. In 1850, Jonathan Whitney, the preacher, found the facility unsuitable, and he urged that they have better place to worship. That year, a building was moved into place opposite the Congregational church. By 1896, the building was in poor condition and was torn down and the Methodists discontinued their services in East St. Johnsbury.

# Catholics

Little is known about the Catholic history prior to 1853. Records show that visiting priests did celebrate Mass, probably in private homes before the erecting of the first church. No records of baptism or marriage were recorded here; perhaps they were recorded in the visiting priest's parish. Land was bought on Cherry Street for the first church on February 27, 1856. In July 1858, Reverend Stanislaus Danielou was named the first pastor of the new parish of Our Lady of Victory. With the title in the English language, it indicates that it was a parish to serve both the French- and English-speaking Catholics. The church was completed and blessed on July 25, 1860. Built of brick, it measured 94 feet long, 40 feet wide and 110 feet from the ground to the top of the cross. In 1859, land was purchased for the Catholic cemetery in Summerville with land near the Passumpsic River and Washington Avenue area. Father Danielou served until 1874, when he went to New Jersey to serve the Catholic faith there.

Father Boissonnault came to the Catholic parish in 1874, taking on the spiritual needs as well as a debt of $12,000. During his thirty-five years there, his accomplishments were many; in May 1876, he purchased land for a new cemetery, as the other had run out of room. This cemetery fronts on the present St. Johns Street. In 1884, a new rectory was needed and property was acquired on Prospect Street. In 1886, when repairs were to be made in the Catholic church on Cherry Street, it was discovered that the foundations were not solid. Coupled with the fact that the church was too small, it was decided to build a new one. In July 1886, the rectory was moved thirty feet to the east on Prospect Street to make room for the foundation of the new church, Notre Dame de Victoire. The architect was George H. Guernsey of Montpelier and the contractor was Dubuc & Belisle dit Lavasseur Company of St. Albans, Vermont. The site is referred to in the *Caledonian* of January 1889:

> *The site, to begin with, is a magnificent one. On the crest of the hill, that rises from the river, the view on the east extends far up the "Moose River" valley and on the north and south the course of "Passumpsic" can be followed for a long distance, and the wooded hills, the winding rivers, and the pleasant fields make the prospect one of surpassing beauty. And for miles east of the village, the church will be a most prominent landmark.*

The new church measured 140 by 65 feet with a tower in the center that rose 198 feet into the air with a 9-foot cross on the top. The seating capacity of this building was 1,200. The entire cost of the church, including electric lights, marble altars and an organ, was $42,611.66. The church was dedicated on the Epiphany of 1889.

The school for boys, St. Gabriels, was established and the convent, Mount St. Joseph for girls, was built. The St. Johnsbury Hospital was begun by Father Boissonnault. Probably the most sorrowful experience was the differences between the Irish and the French Catholics. This resulted in a separation of the two and separate parishes for the Irish- and English-speaking Catholics.

Notre Dame de Victoire.

*Left*: Steeplejack Fred Vermette on the Notre Dame steeple.

*Below*: The funeral procession of Father Boissonnault down Eastern Avenue.

St. Aloysius Catholic
Church, now called St. John
the Evangelist.

This separation would result in the parish of St. Rose, later called St. Aloysius, being established. It is believed that Father Boissonnault destroyed all records and correspondence so that others would not have to know of these troubled times. His death came on March 8, 1909, when he was recognized by both Catholics and Protestants alike. Businesses were closed as his body was taken to burial in a procession down Eastern Avenue and up Railroad to the Catholic cemetery.

In 1916, Father Drouhin had the rectory repaired and remodeled, making it one of the finest rectories around. French Gothic designs were followed so as to be in harmony with the church. The exterior was to be red brick with white cement mortar. The front porch opened into a conservatory.

In 1918, fire destroyed the first church (Our Lady of Victory), now known as St. Agnes Hall on Cherry Street. The second disaster to hit the parish was in April 1920, when the cross atop the steeple of Notre Dame de Victoire was blown down in a high wind.

Father Dame was responsible for Mount St. Joseph Academy High School being accredited by the State Department of Education in 1952. Today, the rectory is a dental building. The Good Shepherd Catholic School has been open on Maple Street since 1998, and the worst change was the fire that consumed the church in 1966.

In 1896, the old Cross Bakery site on Main Street was bought to be the place where the Irish- and English-speaking Catholics would worship. This brick building with a seating capacity of five hundred was dedicated on October 26, 1898. First known as St. Rose, the name was later changed to St. Aloysius. The Knights of Columbus were organized in this parish in 1896. With the fire that destroyed Notre Dame de Victoire, the two parishes were once more joined, and the St. Aloysius Church today is called St. John the Evangelist Catholic Church.

## Universalists

In 1868, the Universalist Church of the Messiah Society was formed. In 1871, Reverend B.M. Tillotson accepted a call as the permanent pastor and served for twelve years. It was under his leadership that a church was erected on Eastern Avenue and dedicated on January 23, 1873. This was another design of Lambert Packard and had a seating capacity of five hundred. In 1972, the front portion of the church was taken down by Rodd the roofer, the owner. A part of the church at the rear, facing Cherry Street, was left standing; it is still an active church.

## Baptists

A Free Will Baptist Church was organized in 1869. In 1875, a church was erected at the corner of Main and Prospect Streets. On Sunday morning, March 26, 1881, this church was reduced to ashes. Generosity from members and nonmembers saw a new building occupied by December 3, 1882. The building was a replica of the one lost and had a seating capacity of three hundred. The Free Will Baptist Church Society gradually ceased, and the church was later taken over by the First Church of Christ Scientist.

The First Baptist Church was organized by William Bacon in 1874. The following year, its members had a church built on Railroad Street. This church could seat 250 and was the only church on Railroad Street and in proximity to Summerville. In 1904, a chapel was added in the rear of the building. The parsonage adjoined the church, and the final addition was the fellowship hall, a combination gymnasium and auditorium with a stage. Today, the building is no longer a church but the Natural Provisions store. The Union Baptist Church moved south of town on Route 5, with a new church and school established in Waterford. The school closed at the end of the 2008–09 school year.

## Advent Christians

In 1875, about forty people formed the Advent Christian Church under the leadership of Reverend M.A. Potter. The following year, a building was erected on Pleasant Street that could seat about four hundred.

## St. Andrew's Episcopal

St. Andrew's Episcopal Church was formally organized in 1876. Meetings were first held in 1856 in the old Union Hall on Main Street and occasionally thereafter prior to 1876. The house of worship was built on Main Street and dedicated on August 3, 1881. The Hook and Hastings pipe organ was given in 1882 by Captain Edward Griswold in memory of his wife, Ellen. The organ had 397 pipes and was powered by a water wheel. Edward was a survivor of the Civil War.

## Presbyterians

July 29, 1879, saw the Reformed Presbyterian congregation organized in St. Johnsbury. In 1883, a house of worship was erected on Eastern Avenue. There were thirty-one members at this time. In 1892, this church was transferred to the Presbyterian General Assembly; three years later, services ceased. The church was made over into a business block and apartments. The lower part served as a pizza place for many years—George's and later Aja's.

The former Presbyterian church on Eastern Avenue. *From* Street, Public Buildings and General Views of St. Johnsbury, Vermont, *published by F.O. Clark.*

## Christian Scientist

The First Church of Christ Scientist was organized on January 26, 1898, and established with bylaws revised by the Mother Church in Boston on October 26, 1900. The Odd Fellows Hall on Railroad Street was used for meetings, as was the Pythian Hall. The congregation later took over the former Free Will Baptist Church on the corner of Main and Prospect Streets. A reading room is located on the lower floor.

## Seventh-Day Adventist

The Seventh-Day Adventist Church is located at 54 Southard Street. The Caledonia Christian School was established in 1952 in the church building.

## Beth-El Synagogue

The organization of the Jewish community might well have started with Marge Iverson, who organized the St. Johnsbury Jewish Women's Club in

1940. This group took care of hospitality, held regular religious studies and gave prayer books on the thirteenth birthdays of its teenage members. On September 22, 1946, the community dedicated the Beth-El Synagogue. Its members met on Railroad Street over McClellan's store. In 1950, Beth-El adopted a constitution that outlined its purposes: to support the upkeep of the synagogue, support the religious education of the Jewish children and pursue social interests and help charitable causes. A new home was needed in 1979, and two rooms were offered at St. John's Catholic community center on Maple Street. The year 1981 saw the breaking of ground on Hospital Drive for their new building. The formal dedication was held on August 22, 1982, with Rabbi Wall of Burlington presiding. In January 1992, Professor Julius Lester became the congregation's lay religious leader. His monthly visits from outside Amherst, Massachusetts, continued until 2002. In 2006, the congregation celebrated twenty-five years in its building and sixty years for the congregation.

## Church Bells

When one looks out over the town, the high points are trees, towers and steeples. Many of the towers and steeples have bells. Some rang out on Sundays, some rang for fires and some rang for the death of a community member. Here are a few of their stories.

The pioneer bell belongs to the old North Church on the Plain. It took about two weeks to get the eight-hundred-pound bell here from Boston by teams of horses, arriving here on a Sunday in 1833. It was hoisted into the tower several days later, and Edward Fairbanks said that there was disappointment in Fairbanks Village, for residents there could not hear it. Adjustments were made and the sound reached them, some said not directly but by the echo reflecting off Crow Hill. This was a busy bell, for it rang at six and nine o'clock in the morning, at noon and at nine o'clock at night. A death was reported by the passing bell—nine strokes for a man, six for a woman and three for a child. When the meetinghouse moved down the street, the bell went to the Methodist church in Concord. It was disabled at the ringing of the announcement of Lee's surrender at Appomattox Court House. In 1896, it was returned to St. Johnsbury and to the scale works, where it was converted into scale beams.

The bell that has rung the longest is the one in East St. Johnsbury, starting in 1842. It hangs in the Third Congregational Church.

The Universalist church in the Center called for a bell in its specifications. This bell rang out for approximately thirty-three years and perished in the fire. The old meetinghouse at the top of the hill had to wait until it had been moved before it received its bell. It was hung in the summer of 1855, and the children of the village school were allowed a break to watch it hoisted into place. It is the only church bell in the village now.

When the second North Church was built in 1847, it had a bell weighing 2,500 pounds that shook the steeple when it was rung. The bell developed a crack on its rim after five years, which did nothing to improve its sound. At the time the South Church was being built, the bell was sent to a foundry and, with added metal, was made into two bells. The congregation had been divided; so too was the bell. Weighing 1,500 pounds and sounding in the key of G, one was hoisted into the South Church, where it called people to worship and sounded the hours on the village clock that was put there in 1853. The other bell, weighing 1,300 pounds and sounding in the key of A, went to the North until the church was moved to make way for the third North Church. The present North Church has a bell weighing 3,004 pounds, sounding in the key of E flat. It entered its Gothic tower in October 1880. Inscribed on the bell are the words: "Unto you, O men I call; And my voice is to the sons of man."

The 1874 Methodist bell had an interesting problem: at 1,400 pounds and sounding in the key of E, it did not harmonize with the other bells. It was exchanged for one sounding in the key of F and weighing 2,100 pounds. The cost was $900, of which the village trustees paid $100 for the right to attach it to the fire alarm.

Notre Dame had three bells consecrated on Sunday, July 2, 1876. The bells were rung for marriages and baptisms when requested. At funerals, they were rung in three different keys, from low to high and then all together. They rang out at 6:00 a.m., noon and 6:00 p.m.

The bell in the Advent Christian Church was presented by Colonel Frederick Fletcher in 1876 at a cost of over $1,000. Fletcher was born in Woodstock, Vermont, the youngest of twelve children. His time was spent in Bridport, Jericho and Burlington before coming to St. Johnsbury during the Civil War. He entered the militia in 1826 and rose to the rank of colonel of the Eighth Regiment. His business success followed him here, as he was a prime mover in establishing the Merchants National Bank in 1875. He was its first president, serving for twelve years.

The Academy bell was hung in 1872. This replaced the old dinner bell that Principal Colby used to shake at the open window during the Academy's early days. The new bell rang at the beginning of school in the morning and afternoon and also after athletic victories.

In 1895, the village trustees placed the fire alarm bell in the courthouse. It would ring out a number that told the location of the fire. It also rang out when court was in session.

A bell used to ring the men to work at the scale factory, from 6:00 a.m. to 6:00 p.m.; it was replaced by the steam gong.

The bell in the tower of the Union Baptist Church came from Essex Junction Baptist Church in 1927. The bell in St. Andrew's Episcopal Church came from a church at Enosburg Falls and was brought here in 1939. It weighs 1,800 pounds and was made in Sheffield, England. At 11:00 a.m. on Sundays it rings nine times—three sets of three notes—signifying the Unity and the Trinity.

There were bells at Summer Street, Portland Street, St. Johnsbury Center and Arlington Schools that are now hung together outside of the St. Johnsbury Town School on Western Avenue. Occasionally, the bells toll for special occasions, the last one being February 12, 2009, marking the 200th birthday of Abraham Lincoln. Bells tolled for ten minutes.

## Mount Pleasant Cemetery

Returning to Mount Pleasant Cemetery, you can find hundreds of former members of some of the churches mentioned. One monument of note is that of Reverend James Johnson, the first pastor of the Second Congregational Church, in 1826. He can be found straight out from the chapel, ten yards down the middle road and to your left. After eleven years, Reverend Johnson was dismissed when "an alienation of a portion of the church from the pastor was discovered." At his dismissal, he still received praise for his fidelity and efforts in building up the church. There were 221 members received into the church during his tenure.

Another grave to visit is that of Lambert Packard, architect for E. & T. Fairbanks and designer of some of the churches, including North Congregational, St. John the Evangelist and the Universalist church, as well as many of the homes in town. He rests on top of the hill that is accessed by the road to the left. As you get close to the peak, keep your eyes to the left and don't look for anything spectacular, for he must not have designed his stone. There is no hint of his abilities on his monument.

The Fletcher monuments can be found by looking north from the Packard stone: one of them is the granite statue of Hope, perhaps the most imposing of all the stones in the cemetery. Colonel Frederick Fletcher's grave is to the left of Hope. Donor of the Advent Christian Church bell, he died in his ninety-fourth year.

# CHAPTER 8

# EDUCATION AND RECREATION

E ducation has always played an important role in New Englanders' lives, and such was the case in St. Johnsbury. The town was originally divided into several school districts, and each district was responsible for its own school. There was no whole town school district until the state legislature passed a law in 1892 that required the whole town to be one district, under one school board. Prior to this, each district chose a prudential committee to oversee the operation of the school, including hiring a teacher, securing the supply of wood, janitor services and other incidentals. At biannual school district meetings, the voters decided how long the next term of school would be; whether to hire a man or a woman; and how payment for the teacher would be provided. They usually bid off the boarding of the teacher to whoever would do it for the least amount of money.

In the early days, two terms made up a school year. One term was for about three months in the summer and three or four months for the winter term. Later, the terms changed to three: fall, winter and spring. Members of the prudential committee were expected to visit the school fairly often to keep an eye on how things were going. They had the power to close a school if it did not seem to be profitable.

One district allowed Bible readings while another district did not. By the time the districts numbered seventeen, one can understand why the legislature voted to have just one district under one school board. Too many variations in ideas and procedures made this necessary.

## Early Schools and Districts

Of all the records that do exist, it would seem that the first building constructed for educational purposes was in the Center (District 5). It was

The ninth-grade class at Summer Street School, 1898. *Courtesy of William Pearl.*

located near the old meetinghouse on the hill. Schools prior to this were held in rooms of private homes. The vote of January 5, 1807, was to have the house built of wood, painted and finished by October of that year. Hiram N. Roberts's narrative in Edward Fairbanks's history of the town describes the schoolhouse this way: "It was not very large, the outside was clapboarded and the inside was sheathed up with wide boards; two rows of seats around, and then a row of seats part way around, and were made of slabs with the flat side up for the little ones to sit on—they were called the Slab Children."

Evidently the stone fireplace did not provide enough warmth, so they improvised. A large kettle that was probably used to make potash was put upside down on a hearth made of stone. A hole was put in the side to take the wood and another hole was made on the top to put a pipe to carry the smoke away. Mention is made of a "School Marm" being paid from eighty cents to a dollar a week, with board, for her work. This building was replaced by one of brick and built right in the Center Village. This was said to be able to accommodate one hundred scholars. A third building in this district was also of brick and had desks, a good blackboard and was heated with a stove. This school building was burned down in 1876.

The Plain District had approximately fifty-four children between the ages of four and eighteen years in 1807. It was voted to build a schoolhouse that was first located halfway up (north) the Plain. This building should have been put on wheels, for it moved quite a bit. It traveled to the north end of the Plain and then down to the burying ground vicinity, followed by a move to where the Colonial Apartments are today. This area was rather wet and on old maps shows a wet gulley extending across the Plain, which was drainage from a swamp or pond in the Summer Street area. One interesting note of the district meeting in 1813 was the vote not to have any needlework or knitting admitted in the school.

One story that is worth passing on of these early school days was the "Judgment Day." In Fairbanks's history, this day was remembered by a daughter whose mother was an early student of St. Johnsbury School. The master of the school appeared quite calm and lenient throughout the school term, but it was noticed that when there were incidents, the master would take out a notebook and write in it. His remark was always that this was for the Judgment Day. The contents of the notebook were revealed on the afternoon of the last day of the school term. The doors were locked and the wooden window shutters were closed and hasped. The master pulled out his book, and students had to atone for their previous actions. The mother who recalled this story was made to stand on the cold stove for fifteen minutes for being tardy. Punishments for girls who giggled or whispered included having their ears twisted and holding weights at arms' length. The boys were punished by having their hands rapped with a wooden ruler or having to remove their jackets for the birch rod treatment. This was rendered for having made mischief with paper wads or bent pins. This "day" was carried out with formality, with the name of the individual called out, the offense read and the punishment delivered.

In 1856, it was voted to build a larger school (District 1) at the corner of Winter and Summer Streets. This school was outgrown rather quickly due to the growth of population with the scale company. The old schoolhouse was moved up Summer Street, where it served as an armory and later a tenement building. A new brick building was dedicated in August 1864. By 1881, it was necessary to provide more room, and in the spring of 1882, it was voted to build a new brick building on the east side of Summer Street. Quicksand was struck there, and another vote was passed to buy property just north of the present building, move the house off and build there. Completed in 1883, this building served until the late 1940s, when it was condemned and torn down. In November 1882, a serious fire occurred in the south building, leaving only the brick shell standing. The fire happened on a Friday morning, and on Monday morning all students were in school in various places. The rebuilding took a little over three months, which was amazing. It stands today as an office building, beautifully preserved with an unobstructed view out to Main Street. The reason for this view is due to the open area being deeded to School District 1 on November 28, 1863, by

Union schools on Summer Street.

Charles S. Dana, Esquire, for consideration of $1,200, "to have and to hold, etc., on condition that no building is erected on any part of said granted premises." In June 1864, the ground was graded and the area was called Central Park. Most often it was referred to as the school common.

District 1 included Fairbanks Village School, located on Mount Vernon Street. Grades one and two were moved into the Trade School in 1942 and that ended the school there.

Other school districts included District 2, which was the area east of Main Street; the first school was put up in 1858 and the second on Maple Street in 1864. It is now owned by the American Legion.

Right about where the Moose and Passumpsic Rivers come together was the Branch Bridge School, on the high ground. This was in existence from about 1810 to 1842. Then District 3 was formed in the Paddock Village area and a school was built on Pleasant Street. Increased numbers saw this school turn into a residence, and a bigger school was built on School Street. The second school was moved to Emerson Street and serves as a residence today, as does the first school. The third school building was erected in 1923 and serves as the Caledonia School today.

District 4 may well have been the first outside district and was known as Four Corners School. District 7 was in that same area and was known as the Goss Hollow School. This was the last of the one-room schools to be closed, in 1949.

District 5 was the Center. District 6 was home to the Spaulding Neighborhood School, located in an area off from Route 2 east, turning by the new location of Fairbanks Scales. This school opened and shut according to need and was sold in 1915

District 8 was known as the Stark District, located northwest of St. Johnsbury Center. It operated into the 1930s. District 9 was Bible Hill, northeast of the Center. The school there was opened as early as 1826, but by the 1900s it was only used part of the time.

District 10 was known as the Chesterfield Hollow District. It was located on the road from East St. Johnsbury to Red Village. Started in 1834, this school was used until the early 1900s, when its students went to East St. Johnsbury. District 13 was East St. Johnsbury. The third building to serve as the school, built in 1911, still stands. It continued as a school until 1979, when it was closed.

District 11, known as Parks District, was a split district with part in Waterford and part in St. Johnsbury. When the law changed in 1892, St. Johnsbury students had to be transported to the Union School. District 12 was Pierce's Mills, up by the present Forest and Stream Club. This school was operational as early as 1814 and burned down in 1899; it was then rebuilt and used into the 1930s.

East St. Johnsbury School.

Portland Street School.

District 14 was the Clay Hill area, now old Route 2. Its schoolhouse was built in the 1840s on the south side of the road, and in 1903 a new school was built on the other side of the road; both are homes now. District 15, once known as Elyville and then Summerville, started in 1842 using the old Branch Bridge School that was moved up there. The third building was known as the Portland Street School; it now serves as the Cornerstone School.

Last but not least, the smallest district was Coles Corner, up in the northwest part of St. Johnsbury. Its schoolhouse was there in 1858 and served into the 1900s off and on as the numbers rose and fell. It was sold in 1947 and just a few years ago was part of a controlled burn that saw all evidence of a school disappearing.

# Trade School

Vocational education started in 1918 in St. Johnsbury. During the First World War, Fairbanks Scales needed skilled workers. Ads indicated the need for two hundred skilled or unskilled workers at the plant. In August 1918, a letter was published in the *Caledonian* from the state director of industrial education urging boys to take advantage of vocational training. On September 3, Fairbanks opened an all-day cooperative school where boys could learn a trade, get a high school education and get paid. This vocational program, opened with twenty boys enrolled, served both students and the Fairbanks Company. The program was made available through the Smith-Hughes Act, with the federal government paying half the expense. Weekly pay was $4.15 for the first year, reaching a high of $8.31 in the fourth year. This start of vocational education would lead to the St. Johnsbury Trade School being built in 1942 and end with the current vocational center in Streeter Hall at the Academy in 1970.

## Consolidation

Bids for building the St. Johnsbury Trade School on Western Avenue on the former Elmwoode site (home of Thaddeus Fairbanks) were opened in January 1941. This structure would replace the Vocational School and Fairbanks Village School. The contractor was D.A. Sullivan & Sons of Northampton, and they were to start on March 1 with a bid of $126,000. Dedication of the building was held on April 22, 1942, with 600 people attending the open house. The school had 115 vocational students and two classrooms for the Fairbanks Village School students.

In November 1950, voters turned out to support the junior high addition to the trade school building. The vote was 1,334 in favor of this $300,000 addition that would house all the seventh and eighth graders in town and also have a gymnasium-auditorium. The nays registered 375. This vote was followed by yet another hurdle: when the bids were opened at the end of April, all were rejected. Problems existed with the amount of steel needed and the number of piles needed to support the gymnasium. Plans changed, and the gym was placed broadside to Western Avenue, utilizing a natural ledge for some of its support. It was also decided to use cream-colored brick over cinder block along with large areas of glass brick. In August 1952, a bid was accepted from Cummings Construction of Woodsville, and work began in November. June 1954 saw the first graduation of 93 graduates from the new junior high.

On July 23, 1968, a third vote was held on the now twice-defeated plan of the Academy housing and running the vocational center. Construction was underway by the start of the 1969–70 school year. This vocational center would be named Streeter Hall after Lewis Streeter, who served as principal of the Trade School for twenty-four years.

In 2000, the trade school—junior high building was transformed once more. Construction took place, and in 2001, all schools came under one roof,

St. Johnsbury Town School. All other remaining public schools—Arlington, Portland Street, Summer Street, Adams and Lincoln Street—closed.

# Parochial Schools

Mount St. Joseph was opened in 1883; this was a boarding school, with the top floor serving as a dormitory. During its history, there were eight grades of regular school and then a two-year commercial course. Later, four years of high school were added. Some students went for eight years at Mount St. Joseph and then four years at the Academy. Mount St. Joseph closed its doors in 1961, and the building was destroyed by fire in 1972.

St. Gabriel's School was for boys and was not a boarding school. It, too, had eight regular grades plus a two-year commercial course. Catholic Central was built in 1961 on Maple Street; it closed in 1971, as did many Catholic schools due to costs. Good Shepherd Catholic School opened in this building in 1998 and is ongoing.

# Recreation

Regardless of the period of history, the amount of work that needed to be done or the amount of time that could be given to relaxation, recreation could always be found in St. Johnsbury in one form or another. Depending on whether you were a participant or a spectator, recreation provided a respite from the work of life.

Turning first to what the winter months provided, skating was and still is a pastime shared by many. The Butler Skating Park was started in 1860, when Beauman Butler graded and flooded eight acres of meadow east of the old road to the Center Village. There was a high fence enclosing the rink, and a small building provided warmth and a lunch counter. The park opened on November 30, 1860, with tickets costing ten cents for each person and season tickets for one dollar. Opening day saw approximately seventy-five skaters and a good group of spectators. The novelty of the safety and attractiveness of this park was outweighed by the distance from the main villages, and it failed after a season or two.

Another early skating spot was the artificial pond in the hollow west of Erastus Fairbanks's home. This pond later was drained and became the lumberyard for the scale company. The Passumpsic River was also used by skaters. It was not the safest, but when the ice was good and the snow was lacking, one could go quite a distance. The year 1895 saw a rink operated by Louis Beaudoin and Louis Gingras on Railroad Street; it offered safe skating with lights. It was in the area now filled in and serving as a parking lot for the Rite Aid drugstore. A 1917 *Caledonian* mentions a skating rink established on the Summer Street Common, and rinks appeared in Arlington's Ramsey Park and across from the Portland Street School. The Summer Street and Portland Street rinks still operate in the winter. In Claire Dunne Johnson's book *I See by the Paper…*, mention is made that John Belknap was making good-quality skates in 1860.

Tobogganing was gaining in popularity, and in 1885 it was noted that Burlington had a toboggan chute, so why not St. Johnsbury? This would wait until 1887, when one was built on the Carpenter lot at the head of the Plain, running behind the Main Street houses to the school common. It was 40 feet high and 160 feet long and was built by A.L. Bragg in January at a cost of $300. It was constructed so that it could be taken down at the end of the season and put back the following winter. The Caledonia Toboggan Club announced that the chute would open from 2:00 to 6:00 p.m. and 7:00 to 10:00 p.m. every day except Wednesday and maybe Sunday. For $3, a season ticket admitted one man and lady. A single admission was $0.25. The Academy had a half holiday the first Monday it was open, with Principal Putney and other teachers joining in. Despite the Carpenter family wanting the chute down and the fact that lots for houses were starting to be opened

Summer Street skating rink.

The toboggan chute at the head of Clinton Avenue.

up in the area, the chute was put up for another year. Enthusiasm had waned by this time, however, and the chute was open only three days a week. In April 1888, it was taken down for the final time. James Ritchie, a member of the YMCA, read this original poem at the Y banquet:

> *Tobogganing*
> *Toboggan slides as we all know,*
> *Are only built when there's plenty of snow.*
> *Some are made by kind nature's hand,*
> *But ours is built on Carpenter's land.*
>
> *It starts erected forty feet high,*
> *Down which the tobogganists swiftly fly,*
> *Some with suits of blue and gold,*
> *Others whose suits are rusty and old.*
>
> *To slide on a toboggan, Oh! What fun,*
> *Come let's get on, both old and young,*
> *And down the chute at lightning speed—*
> *Oh! To slide on a toboggan is fun indeed.*

*On behalf of the members I wish to extend*
*A cordial invitation for all to attend;*
*It's the latest popular amusement of the day*
*And surely ought to be popular with the Y.M.C.A.*

The St. Johnsbury Snow Shoe Club was a success, with long tramps taken in the evenings. The numbers dwindled with the Great War but climbed back with the formation of the St. Johnsbury Winter Sports Club. Dr. Dale S. Atwood, in the *Vermonter* magazine of 1922, speaks to the success of the club. Its first project was the revitalization of the skating rink on Summer Street Common. It took fifteen hours of spraying the area in below-zero conditions for a firm foundation. Twin State Electric Company men climbed the elms to illuminate the rink. The issue of Sunday skating was addressed, with every one of the churches agreeing to Sunday skating but not during worship hours. Rules barred racing, snapping-the-whip and hockey playing. A hockey club did get established, but some residents played during restricted hours late on some evenings.

The club members proceeded with plans to have a toboggan chute once again. The site chosen was a hillside along an unused road to Observatory Knob. If tobaggoners mastered the ride, they would end up in the golf links—a good half mile away from their starting point. It was steep and faced south, and it was soon discovered that the sun would make it too sticky. So plan B was formed. Behind the clubhouse at the golf links, they made a successful track. The finished rut was nineteen inches at the base, twenty-three inches wide at the top and sixteen inches high. What a ride!

Snowshoe enthusiasts met in front of the Athenaeum in the evening and followed the leader into the darkness. The leader and the end person each had an oil torch. The Devil's Slide was in a far corner of the golf links, and people did not usually end up on their feet. A supper and a dance were usually held at the end of the hike.

Dr. Atwood tells of Main Street being the scene for winter horse races. Road machines made the snow paths for the horses. Saturdays would see many spectators watching these races. They started at Arnold Park, with the finish opposite the museum. An electric bell signal from the starters allowed for perfect timing of the heats.

On certain evenings, some of the steep streets, like Pleasant, Concord Avenue and Hastings, were given over to police protection of the traverse riders. Some of these double-runner sleds would hold ten to twelve people, which made for momentum. Sometimes there was a steering wheel as opposed to just ropes for steering. The scooter or jumper was also popular. It

Old Pine golf links, Overclyffe.

had one runner that curled at the front. A couple of braces supported a seat with grooved handgrips underneath. Feet lifted, riders leaned backward with balance maintained for as long as they could.

The Old Pine and Observatory Knob were also runs for skiers. Weekend ski runs were held, with lodging made at a farmhouse and skiers returning the following day.

When there was no snow, there was golf. In 1899, the high pasturelands to the right of Underclyffe were set aside for a golf course. This was about twenty acres and was laid out by Alex Findlay, considered to be the champion golfer of the time. Alex was hired by Frank Brooks, who occupied Underclyffe mansion with his wife, Ellen Fairbanks. He laid out a course of nine holes ranging from 100 to 260 feet apart. He was quite happy with the layout, as he said it combined hazards and long drives up and down the hillside. Known as the Old Pine Golf Club, the name was for the old pine that stood for years at the top of the land. In 1902, the golf course had a clubhouse built of 16- by 30-foot dimensions. At the southwest corner of the grounds, adjoining the clubhouse, a tennis court was constructed. Nothing lasts forever, and in 1923, the organization of the St. Johnsbury Country Club came into being. The Morrill farm was purchased at the north edge of St. Johnsbury on the road to Lyndonville. In 1923, Willie Park Jr. designed the nine-hole course. In 1924, the club hired an expert, Robert Dobson, formerly from

Riverside Canoe Club, Passumpsic River.

England. He had played golf all his life and had five years as a golf pro; he charged one dollar for a half-hour lesson. In 1927, major improvements had been made to the clubhouse, renovating it from a farmhouse to a modern clubhouse. In 1992, nine more holes were added to the course.

Canoe enthusiasts formed the Riverside Canoe Club in May 1908, with fifteen to eighteen members. Canoes could be rented for the five-mile round trip to the Center and back. On Memorial Day 1912, three canoeists lost their lives, with one surviving. The Passumpsic River was swollen and Mr. Clark would not let two ladies, Helen Smythe and Helen Ellis, rent a canoe alone. He let Lewis Kimball and Herbert Smythe rent the canoe later that day along with the ladies. All was well until they approached the rapids just above Hastings Bridge. The canoe swerved and overturned, dumping everyone. Lewis Kimball was the only survivor. The canoe club continued until 1927, when the flood washed it away.

Observatory Knob was the height of land between the Passumpsic and Sleepers Rivers, northwest of the village. Charlie Hastings was awed by the panoramic view that it gave and wanted all to enjoy it. The Presidential Range, Mount Moosilauke, Burke Mountain and Willoughby were all part of the view. Hastings had the idea of putting a small observatory on top of Preston's hill (about a half mile west of the Mount Pleasant Cemetery). In 1887, Charlie Hastings put out a plea through the *Caledonian* for volunteers with hammers, saws and paintbrushes to erect this observatory. He equipped the observatory with rests for telescopes and spy glasses. The Knob became a favorite spot for an outing. Hiram Turner became the owner of some of the land, and he personally set out maple trees along the carriage road, which was built in 1889. Horse sheds were erected near the summit, creating a place to park the horse. In October 1894, high winds blew the observatory over. It was replaced the following year with a larger structure. In January 1914, high winds took it down again, and it was not replaced. Now trees have replaced the view it gave.

In 1927, the Rotary Club looked into a swimming pool idea. A committee was appointed to explore the idea of a pool at Emerson Falls. Explore was all that came of it, for it was deemed to be too costly and not very centrally located. In 1931, the Kiwanis Club looked into the swimming pool idea again, including possibly building a dam on the Sleepers River near the Gilman Bros. Property (where the interchange of I-91 exits for Danville). The committee recommended that it would cost at least $300, but the plan was put on hold. The search continued in 1942, with the next idea being the use of land in back of the trade school, which already had a pond. This was the "duck pond," a part of Elmwoode; the pond was drained so that the base could be studied. This pond was fed by a series of springs, but if it were to be acceptable as the pool, it would have to use village water. Success was had, and the groundbreaking ceremony was held in early October. The Kiwanis Club put in $500 to get things going and the Elks Club added $600. Located on Barker Avenue, a clay foundation, gravel fill and good drainage made way for a seventy-five- by one-hundred-foot main pool with a twenty- by forty-foot wading pool.

July 23, 1944, was the dedication of the pool. Virginia Kimball was to be the first supervisor, and swimming lessons were offered two mornings a week. Admission charges for the use of the pool were set for the rest of the season: family, $2.42; adults, $1.60; and students, $0.80. In 1951, to help with the costs of operating the swimming pool, Kiwanis leased the pool to the town so an appropriation of $2,000 could be part of the town budget. The Kiwanis Club has remained dedicated to this pool both in labor and fundraising, with events such as its annual Kiwanis Radio Auction.

The year 1952 saw quite a bit of sports activity for the youth of St. Johnsbury. The winter of 1951–52 was the year that the Rotary Basketball League was started for grades six through eight. The Rotary Club still maintains its interest in basketball, with a yearly Rotary Basketball Tournament. Dr. William Robinson proposed that St. Johnsbury get involved with Little League baseball for boys ages eight through twelve. A public meeting was held at Fuller Hall to explain the program to the townspeople, and $625 of the needed $750 was pledged that night. Accepted by Little League, the program started and continues in St. Johnsbury at this time. There are ball fields located left off from Concord Avenue, just east of Fred Mold Park, three at Leonard Field and two off from Elm Street at Legion Field.

St. Johnsbury has a recreation department whose mission it "is to provide a diverse recreational program which enhances the quality of life for area youth, adults, and senior citizens." The recreation department was housed in the armory (no longer used by the military) until recently. The armory is in need of major repairs at the present time and is no longer an option for the home of the department until decisions are made. At this writing, the recreation department works out of the St. Johnsbury Town School.

## Town Band

The St. Johnsbury Band was founded in 1830, making it the nation's third oldest band in continuous service. Only the West Point Military Band of 1827 and the Allentown, Pennsylvania band of 1829 are older. The band has had several different names; originally known as the Brass Band, it became the Cornet Band, followed in 1885 by the Serenade Band and finally, in 1912, the St. Johnsbury Consolidated Band. The Consolidated Band was a result of the joining of two bands; back in 1880 another band, known as the Harmony Band, had formed. The two bands had to borrow players from each other to keep going, so they finally merged in 1912. The name was shortened to St. Johnsbury Band in 1926. As the name has changed, so have the locations where the band has played. It was first in Arnold Park; another bandstand was in Railroad Street Park and a third was in Courthouse Park. The Railroad Street bandstand was torn down in 1951, and the one in Courthouse Park was torn down in 1952. In 1956, the town appropriated money to build a new bandstand in Courthouse Park. During the time that it lacked a bandstand, the band played one season at Brantview, two seasons on the trade school grounds and one season on the walk at Courthouse Park.

Until 1943, this was an all-male band, but World War II took twenty-two of its members. The director called on the St. Johnsbury Academy Band to fill those empty seats, and twelve girls filled in. Since then, women have been an integral part of the band. The band has played for one president and one former president. The first was for Benjamin Harrison. He was escorted in a parade to Colonel Franklin Fairbanks's Underclyffe home in

St. Johnsbury Band, 1907. *Courtesy of Dianne Rolfe.*

1891. In 1912, former president Theodore Roosevelt was in the audience of a concert at the courthouse. The St. Johnsbury Band currently plays weekly summer concerts in Courthouse Park in the summer, contributes to the town's celebrations and can always be counted on to support the musical needs of the town's institutions.

BAND —

One monument in Mount Pleasant Cemetery gives a hint of a former band member. The French monument has a music lyre on the stone with the inscription:

*Music when soft voices die*
*Vibrates in the memory*

Both Ted and Marion French were musical, with Ted being a longtime member of the band, for which he played trumpet and then baritone horn. This monument can be found by taking the left-hand road by the chapel, proceeding up the hill to the "tub" and going right with an eye to the left just a quarter of the way around the circle.

# CHAPTER 9

# SERVICE TO COUNTRY AND CEMETERIES

Every town has contributed patriotic acts and deeds during the wars that have affected this country. St. Johnsbury has records and monuments that point to its contributions in times of war. In times of greatest troubles, people rally and come together in all sorts of ways; so goes St. Johnsbury.

## Civil War

At the time of the fall of Fort Sumter on April 14, 1861, which would lead the country into the Civil War, Erastus Fairbanks was governor of the state of Vermont. On April 15, President Lincoln called for seventy-five thousand troops, of which Vermont was to furnish one regiment. And so it was that the first official document of the war was issued from St. Johnsbury on April 15, 1861, by Governor Fairbanks. The second paragraph reads:

*Now, therefore, I, Erastus Fairbanks, Governor of the State of Vermont, by virtue of the authority vested in me by the Constitution, do hereby issue my Proclamation for convening the General Assembly in an extra session; and I do hereby summon the members of the Senate and House of Representatives to meet together in their respective Chambers at Montpelier together with the officers of the two houses, on Tuesday the twenty-third day of April, instant, at ten o'clock, A.A., for the purpose of adopting measures for organizing, arming and equipping the Militia of the State, and for co-operating effectually with the General Government in suppressing insurrection and executing the laws.*

*Given under my hand and the seal of the State at St. Johnsbury, this fifteenth day of April, in the year of our Lord one thousand eight hundred and sixty-one, and of the Independence of the United States the Eighty Fifth.*

Feeling for the preservation of the United States ran high, and St. Johnsbury showed this spirit in a patriotic rally held on April 16 at the St. Johnsbury Town Hall, which was filled to overflowing. The proclamations of President Lincoln and Governor Fairbanks were read and resolutions for support of the government and the flag of the Union were adopted. This was followed on April 19 by a patriotic band concert with additional speeches. Monday, April 22, saw yet another rally with speeches by Honorable Charles Dana, Judge Luke Poland and the governor. At this rally, seventy men gave their names in writing as volunteers for the military.

That same week, on April 27, the Ladies' Aid Association was organized at the town hall, with approximately 150 ladies pledging their support for aid and comfort that they might provide for the soldiers. The following is part of the resolutions that they passed to economize:

> *We, the ladies of St. Johnsbury, will retrench our individual expenses and will purchase during the coming season only calico or low priced muslin for dresses unless for some special reason other material should be required. We will also observe the same economy in all our apparel, laying aside costly gloves and purchasing plain bonnets and no unnecessary articles whatever.*

The ladies of St. Johnsbury also made up a regimental flag that was sixteen by eight feet in size. It was formally presented through the hand of the governor on July 4. This patriotic day began with a thirty-four-gun salute fired from the twelve-pounder on the bluff south of the Plain overlooking Camp Baxter. The salute was followed by the ringing of the village bells for about a half hour, repeated at noon and sundown.

Visitors entering St. Johnsbury from Route 5 north will pass by a boulder with a marker and flag marking Camp Baxter, first campsite of the Third Regiment, which was located on the old fairgrounds. I-91 has replaced what was known as Hazen Field and the location of the old fairgrounds. The soldiers were not in tents but in the main building on the ground, which was extended to a length of 340 feet, with three-tiered bunks for one thousand men. Through the center of this building ran dining tables. Additional buildings were put up for the culinary department, hospital needs and the Camp Baxter Post Office. Camp Baxter was named for Adjutant and Inspector General Baxter.

The Third Regiment was mustered into service on July 16 with 882 men and a band of 24 players. They left on July 24 in a train of twenty-two cars. The Third would participate in twenty-eight engagements, including Antietam, Wilderness Campaign, Gettysburg, Cold Harbor, Petersburg,

Winchester, Spotsylvania and Fredericksburg. They lost heavily in killed and wounded. Other men from town served in the Tenth, Eleventh, Fourth, Fifth, Sixth, Eighth, Ninth, Twelfth, Fifteenth and Seventeenth Regiments. They also served in the First Regiment Cavalry, First Battery Light Artillery and Second Regiment Sharpshooters.

Located throughout the older sections of Mount Pleasant Cemetery can be found victims of the Civil War, casualties and survivors of that terrible strife. We learn of their service through a book, *St. Johnsbury Soldiers' Record*, compiled by Honorable Albert G. Chadwick. He was directed to prepare this record by a vote of the town on March 7, 1865. This was accomplished in 1883 and contained the records of 374 men of the town. Straight out from the chapel at the cemetery we find John Green, who served in Company A, Eleventh Regiment. He mustered into service on September 1, 1862. He was taken prisoner on June 23, 1864, at Weldon Railroad and taken to Andersonville, Georgia. He was confined there for five months, after which he became a patient of the Naval School Hospital in Annapolis, Maryland, where he died on December 5, 1864, from the effects of disease that he contracted from prison. There is a Green Street off from present-day Main Street named for this family.

Taking the middle road straight out to our landmark spruce, you find the stone marking the Ripley family. Lieutenant John Ripley is so marked, and from his dates you know that he survived the war. An interesting and very sad story can be told here. He enlisted in Company C, Eighth Regiment, on November 3, 1861. According to the *Soldiers' Record*, he rose in rank from corporal in 1862 to second lieutenant in February 1864. A few years ago, a call was received from a Southerner who had purchased letters written from a John Ripley to his wife Rhoda in St. Johnsbury. One of John's letters told of terrible news: he had been told by a fellow comrade that his two daughters had died and he was begging his wife to tell him the fate of their son. Well over one hundred years later, the purchaser of these letters was trying to find out the fate of the third child. Locating the Ripley lot, you read that Sevelia, age five, died on March 21, 1863, and Lillie died two days later at age three. No record is found on the stone of a son. The rest of the story is that the son lived and is buried in another cemetery to the north.

Continuing on that same road just a short distance, the road forks; stay right and walk straight ahead and you will find a rather nice white monument marking the grave of Lieutenant Colonel George Chamberlain. Inscribed on the stone is the incident that mortally wounded him. He was leading Company A, Eleventh Regiment, in a skirmish with the Rebels near Charlestown, Virginia. Hit by a musket ball in the abdomen, he fell from his

George Chamberlain monument,
Mount Pleasant Cemetery.

horse; the next day he passed away at a hospital in Sandy Hook, Virginia. Chamberlain had been a graduate of St. Johnsbury Academy and followed that with graduation from Dartmouth College with distinction in 1860. The Grand Army of the Republic (GAR) formed after the war named its St. Johnsbury post Chamberlain Post in honor of George Chamberlain.

Leaving Chamberlain and backtracking about three yards, go right and follow the lower road. At the end of the terrace, you will start up the hill and about midway on the left, crossing over the Crosby lot, you find L.B. Soper at the end of the short terrace. The *Record* tells us that he is Lafayette B. Soper and he enlisted into Company A, Eleventh Regiment, on August 7, 1862. Sergeant Soper was in all actions of the Eleventh Regiment and escaped unharmed until the last engagement. On the side of the stone, it is engraved that Comrade Soper lost a leg at Petersburg, Virginia. The *Record* notes that on April 2, 1865, the front ranks of the Rebels on the south of Petersburg were assaulted by the North and carried. The Rebels were pursued, and "at a point some three miles from their works, Sergeant Soper with Lieutenant John S. Wilson, of Company I with two others, were taking three rebels from a barn. They were in advance of their own line, and were fired upon by their comrades from flank and rear, the seven mingled together being all taken for rebels." Sergeant Soper was struck by a musket ball, shattering his ankle bone. Taken to a hospital, the wound was amputated about four inches above the ankle. And so it goes throughout this cemetery and others, but

Civil War monument, Courthouse Park.

the stories in the *St. Johnsbury Soldiers' Record* help portray the details of these men's roles in the war.

At a special town meeting held on June 23, 1866, a plan was presented for a monument that would honor all the soldiers of the town. Selectmen were instructed to raise a sum not to exceed $10,000. Negotiations were made with Larkin G. Mead Jr., a native of Vermont, to furnish a suitable marble statue. It would be carried out in his studio in Florence, Italy, and delivered to New York City for the sum of $5,000. Peter B. Laird of West Danville was contracted to supply a granite foundation and pedestal for the monument to rest on. The base and pedestal rise twelve feet from the ground. Each side of the pedestal has a shield, and within each shield are the names of those who gave their lives in the war. The monument is from a plan executed by

GAR soldiers monument, Mount Pleasant Cemetery.

architect E. Grebble of Philadelphia. The statue *America* reached this country in the summer of 1868 and was celebrated on August 20. *America* stood seven and a half feet tall and was placed at the north end of the courthouse. The monument was erected at a cost of $8,892.46. This would be the first war monument in Courthouse Park.

The following year, two Parrott guns were added on either side of the monument. The guns were presented to the Chamberlain Post No. 1 of the GAR by the secretary of the navy at the request of General W.W. Grout. The one on the west side of the monument was in service during the Civil War on USS *Magnolia*, and on the east side, the USS *Kanawha*.

In 1957, the Civil War monument was given a face-lift. At the town meeting of that year, it was voted to clean, repair and resurface the monument. The original base had the names hand cut and the restoration was to have the sandblast method used.

In March 1893, it was announced that the Chamberlain Post of the GAR was having a monument made by the Carrick brothers for its lot in the cemetery. It would be a granite six-foot figure of a soldier at rest standing on a six-foot base. The cost was about $400. This soldier can be found by taking the road to the right, going to the top of the long hill, turning right and following down on the right before you get to the Ide monument.

# Armory

In April 1916, it was announced that the State Armory Board was to build an armory for Company D, First Vermont Infantry. At the time, seventy-three men and three officers made up this company. The property that was the most suitable for this was known as the Burnham property on Main Street, between what was known as the Union Block and the Episcopal church. This was purchased by the town and deeded to the state, with the condition that the space might be used for town meetings and voting if needed. Prior to this, Company D had moved about fairly frequently; it had been in Bertrand's Hall building on Railroad Street, the Stanley Opera House, which burned down, and the YMCA after 1914. The Burnham property had four buildings that had to be bought and moved. One was moved to Green Street and the other three went to Harvey Street. Cummings Construction Company was the contractor, and the company went to work after properties were moved and finished in time for a grand ball on February 20, 1917. This would be the site for more dances over time.

# World War I

World War I had been going on for a couple of years before it impacted St. Johnsbury. In April 1917, the National Guard Troops of Vermont were all mobilized. Company D was sent to Charlotte, North Carolina, in July. Patriotism was very evident in St. Johnsbury, beginning with a "Wake Up America" parade with some 3,000 participants. May 23 saw the call for all men between the ages of twenty-one and thirty to register for the draft on June 5. A little over 700 men registered; 2 of the first ones to go from town were Willard Ward and Bill McDonald. A Liberty Bond drive was started. Shortages existed in town, including sugar, flour, newsprint and coal. By July 1918, St. Johnsbury had 288 residents in the army and navy. Spanish influenza hit the troops at Fort Devens as well as the town, and this was still going on when the official news of the war being over arrived on November 11, 1918. The number of flu cases numbered a total of 2,984 in St. Johnsbury. The war ending was marked with a parade and schools closing early to participate. The total participation from town was 401 in the army, 56 in the navy, 5 in the marine corps and 6 in the army nurse corps. A total of 17 lost their lives, while 40 were wounded.

The July 4 celebration of 1921 was quite a festive day that included the dedication of a new World War I memorial. Paid for only by donations, the monument would face Main Street with a height of seven feet, nine inches and a width of eight feet. On this same day in Railroad Street Park, a twelve-foot cannon was mounted on a granite base, having been obtained by the GAR. On the eve of this celebration, a big Canadian bomber plane made several flyovers of the town.

# World War II

In 1941, mobilization came again to Company D; orders were issued for departure to Camp Blanding, Florida. March 12 saw a great sendoff, with the company marching to the railroad station led by the St. Johnsbury Town Band. There, the 120 members boarded a special fourteen-car train. In Florida, they would become part of the Forty-third Division. The town itself was gearing up for the possibilities of all-out war on several fronts. Emergency defense was being coordinated among doctors and nurses; highway and water department workers were working together. Scrap aluminum was collected by Boy Scouts in town and village trucks. Motorists were asked to save 20 percent on their gas consumption. By

August, the St. Johnsbury Civilian Defense group was fully organized, the first in the state.

The year 1942 saw increased impact of the war on residents, including shortages of rubber and sugar. Air raid precautions were handed out and salvage drives were conducted that included paper, scrap metal and rubber. The first of the war ration books came at the end of April. The first of these was issued for sugar, and in the beginning each person was entitled to one pound of sugar every two weeks. Gas rationing cards followed; some foods were scarce due to the shortages of cans. Canned meats, tuna and pineapple were among those in short supply, and later coffee was rationed. The scrap metal drives ended some ornamental features in town, including the fence at the Elks home and the fountain in front of the South Church that had stood there since 1881. Academy students organized a huge search for scrap metal—the second largest in the state—that netted sixty-three tons for their efforts.

The first St. Johnsbury casualty was Roy Proia, killed in a jeep accident at Fort Devens. The first naval casualty was Leo Paul Perrier, lost in the sinking of the USS *Truxton*. The year 1943 brought more restrictions, including public buildings having to convert to coal for heating. The Victory Gardens increased due to the restrictions on food; the Peck Company was the center for finding available garden plots. The St. Johnsbury Women's Club arranged for an Honor Roll billboard in Courthouse Park. The chamber of commerce bought a service flag to suspend across Railroad Street that would show the number of men in the service. In November of this year, it was reported that there were 848 men and women in the service—one tenth of the population.

On August 15, 1945, at 7:00 p.m., the end of the war was announced. There was a rather wild five-hour celebration that followed, with cars and people parading up and down the main streets, horns blaring and firecrackers exploding. H. Guy Dunbar's sound system bus drove around sounding marches at full volume.

On Memorial Day 1955, a nine-foot marble monument was unveiled and dedicated to those community members who lost their lives in World War II. Forty-four names were inscribed on the center column. The monument was sponsored and erected by the St. Johnsbury American Legion Post.

Courthouse Park bears remembrances of all St. Johnsbury's sons and daughters who served in the defense of the country in all wars on Memorial Day of every year.

# Burial Grounds

Burial grounds seem not to have been thought out for the long term and for future generations; in some cases, their locations have been changed entirely and the grounds were no longer used after the graves were relocated to a bigger area. In other instances, the small one remains but another larger one is located elsewhere.

Such was the case with the burial ground beside the church in the Center Village. This one dates back to 1800, with the first burial being that of a boy, son of Joseph Vincent, in 1801. Names of the early burials were well known to the earliest of settlers. Some residents moved the remains of their family members when a new burying ground was opened to the north of the village in 1850. Included in the transfers were three Revolutionary soldiers: Joel Roberts, Simeon Cobb and Jonas Flint. Since the newer cemetery opened, there have been no new burials in the old ground. The present St. Johnsbury Center Cemetery is situated half a mile above the village on a hillside overlooking the Passumpsic River. An association was formed in 1864 to ensure the keeping of the cemetery. In the East St. Johnsbury area, the original burying ground was located on the slope of the hill on the west; in 1857, grounds outside the village overlooking the Moose River were bought for $600. Removals were made from the original site to this cemetery. A receiving vault was constructed and $300 was spent for a village hearse.

Another smaller cemetery, referred to as Goss Hollow Cemetery, is located approximately three miles up Mount Pleasant Extension Road. Here are located members of the Hawkins, Ayers and Goss families.

# Mount Calvary Cemetery

Two of the larger cemeteries are Mount Calvary and Mount Pleasant Cemetery. The first Catholic burial place was on a hillside between Caledonia Street and the Passumpsic River. This land was purchased in 1859 and used until 1876, when $3,000 was spent to obtain a new area for the Catholics to use as their cemetery. The land was located on the Plain above Paddocks Village, now known as Pleasant Street and St. John Street. The bodies were removed from the original burial ground and reburied. Dedication was in October 1876, with a procession of about 1,500 people from Notre Dame de Victoire Church. A memorial was erected in the center of the grounds in 1911: a group of figures represents the virgin mother and St. John with the kneeling Magdalene, above which rises the Savior on the cross. The figures are of bronze and were bought from France.

# Mount Pleasant Cemetery

As mentioned earlier, the first burial ground in town was unsightly and not nearly big enough, not to mention that the area was desired for the courthouse. To address this problem, on May 20, 1851, the St. Johnsbury Cemetery Association was organized. James K. Colby served as the first president while Ephraim Jewett served as the secretary. The charter provided for an issue of one hundred shares at $6 a share. Seventy-eight subscribers took ninety-seven shares, and the name adopted was Mount Pleasant Cemetery. In 1852, eight acres were bought from Lambert Hastings for $450, which included the area nearest the gate. That same year, a strip was gotten from Ephraim Jewett's pasture adjoining the highway farther north. More land was purchased from Lambert Hastings the next year. The grounds were laid out by J.H. Sackett, landscape architect of Springfield, Massachusetts, in the spring of 1853. The dedication services were held on June 2, 1853. The first lot was sold to Ephraim Jewett. Fairbanks, in his history, quotes the

The entrance to Mount Pleasant Cemetery. *Courtesy of William Pearl.*

*Lowell Citizen* of 1875: "Mount Pleasant Cemetery is among the best in New England outside suburban districts; commanding hill and dale, lawn and woodland in happy combination, and has a natural observatory from the summit with charming outlook over the town, the river, the mountains and the verdant valley of the Passumpsic."

In 1870, a receiving vault and pavilion were constructed by E. & T. Fairbanks for the sum of $2,955. In July 1897, the cemetery association voted to build a house and barn for the superintendent of the cemetery. This was to be done for the approximate cost of $3,000. The designer of the house was Lambert Packard. In May 1898, it was announced that the building had been constructed for $2,800 and was almost ready for occupancy. In 1922, the pavilion was being filled in for use as a chapel. This was intended for use for services, if need be, but today its primary purpose is to serve as the office for the cemetery and crematory. The crematory was added in 1966, the first in Vermont. William Pearl, superintendent of the cemetery for thirty-five years, was an advocate of the crematory, and Verner Lurchin, member of the board, left funds to carry out this idea. These burial grounds house the remains of some of the earliest settlers and continue on with present-day deaths, but, old or new, every stone has a story.

# CHAPTER 10

# FIRES AND FLOODS

In the early days, St. Johnsbury fires were fought relying on volunteer bucket brigades that were formed from the water source to the fire. Lines were started from the nearest cistern or near one of the three rivers, if that happened to be closer to the source of the fire. Cisterns filled by rainwater were located throughout the town; one was in the southwest corner of the Summer Street school common and another was on Eastern Avenue. There was no other system until the St. Johnsbury Aqueduct Company was formed in 1860 by its owners, the E. & T. Fairbanks Company. This came about when the Stiles Pond water system was developed.

## Fire Companies

On April 19, 1844, the Franklin Fire Company was started in the old Fairbanks Village schoolhouse. Most of its twenty members were employees of the scale company. In 1853, the Franklin Fire Company reorganized under the Torrent Fire Company, No. 1. While the Torrent had been bought by the E. & T. Fairbanks Company to protect the scale company, it was always under the control of the village. It was hauled to every fire, sometimes by many men clinging to a rope and pulling it up Western Avenue but more often by a pair of horses. The Torrent and, later, a horse cart were stored near the main gate of the factory. At the same time that the Torrent Co. 1 was being formed, there was a group gathered for protection on the Plain forming the Deluge Co. 2. Its members built an engine house on Summer Street, at the girls' common area. Other companies were formed, including the Island Hose Company (Paddock Village), Fletcher Co. 4, Flanders Co. 5 (Railroad Street) and Summerville Co. 6. In 1860, the Torrent made a new appearance with a brand-new engine. According to Arthur Stone, "The tub

Auto Combinations No. 1 Fire Department, St. Johnsbury, Vermont.

was 23 feet long, built of mahogany and rosewood, inlaid with pearl, and with silver lettering." The first foreman of the Torrent Fire Company was Asa Blunt (a colonel in the Civil War) and for many years another foreman was Franklin Fairbanks.

In 1876, the village waterworks were established on the island at the Paddock Village dam. Seventy hydrants were placed from this setup. In 1880, the first fire alarm system was in operation, consisting of six boxes. The bell rang in the Methodist church tower; later, it would ring out at the courthouse. There were four locations of fire equipment: one at the Fairbanks plant, another at Paddocks Village, one on Main Street and the final located on Railroad Street. In 1897, the idea of a central fire station was considered. This station was first established in 1912 on Eastern Avenue where the old post office is today. In 1924, the fire station took up residence on Main Street, where it is at the present time. The present-day location has the big problem of space and how to fit everything in.

In 1934, two storage tanks capable of holding half a million gallons of water each were added at Overclyffe.

# Fires

Noteworthy fires over the years include, in 1858, the old Hezekiah Martin house on Main Street, just north of the present-day Summer Street Common. This was a fine residence, very much like the brick home of Judge Paddock, having been built in 1825 by the same builder. The hall that was attached to this home housed the St. Johnsbury Female Academy for its seventeen-year existence. In 1866, the Railroad Repair Shops burned, taking the machine shop, the blacksmith shop and wood shop with it. This fire threatened the freight and passenger stations and also partially burned one of the first locomotives, called the "Caledonia."

The year 1876 saw two significant fires; one was on January 21 at the scale factory. A cinder fell into a vat of japan (lacquer), which resulted in a fire that threatened the whole complex due to a stiff wind from the west. A special train from Lyndonville brought relays of firemen. All the hydrants, two steam pumps and two engines poured water on the fire. The loss was estimated to be around $40,000; despite the loss, new shops were up and running in just seven weeks. These shops were built with four brick fire walls from sixteen to twenty inches thick. This fire was followed by another on July 1 in the Center Village. Prior to the fire, the village had eighty homes, three churches and several stores, mills or shops. By noon, twenty-seven buildings were gone—a third of the village. There was no telegraph, so a messenger had to ride a horse to the Plain and then the engines were dragged the three miles to get to the fire.

On Main Street in March 1881, the Free Baptist Church was lost on the site of the present-day Christian Scientist church. Railroad Street would be the scene of several huge and deadly fires over the years. In October 1892, the east side of Railroad Street was a roaring inferno, helped by a fierce wind from the north. A roaring noise was heard from Lougee & Smythe's, followed by an explosion, and within a half hour the entire row of business blocks south were on fire. Drouin's, Caldbeck's, Daniels', Merchants Bank, Ward's, Griswold and Pearl's were taken. Thirty families were burned out and two people lost their lives in the Caldbeck Block. When these blocks were built back, Mr. Caldbeck had a statue of Hope erected over the main entrance to the memory of James Mitchell, an employee of Caldbecks' whose life was lost.

January 26, 1896, saw the Passumpsic House–Avenue House destroyed by fire. Thaddeus Spencer, a popular merchant, lived at the house. He successfully got out but went back to retrieve some of his belongings. He inhaled fire and smoke trying to get out the second time and died a few days

The aftermath of the Citizens Bank Block fire, 1909.

later. The wonder of this fire was that it did not destroy the Opera House on Eastern Avenue.

Across the street from the New Avenue House in October 1909, the Citizens Bank Block went up in smoke. Fire was discovered in the basement and destroyed the whole of the interior of this block, taking nine lives. One problem at this fire was that ladders could not reach the heights needed. It is hoped that this record of lives lost will not be broken.

East St. Johnsbury suffered structural losses with the fire in August 1907 that destroyed the old Squire Harrington house, where the Gates family had lived. Another fire destroyed an 1831 store, granary and the Shasteny house. In May 1926, a fire destroyed the cider and bobbin mills, along with the covered bridge in the center of the village. The bridge was on what was then the main road to Concord; it was not in very good shape, so the fire provided a good excuse to replace it.

The Grace Methodist Church was destroyed by fire on January 14, 1915. This very same church had been damaged in a fire in 1908. After the first fire, a fireproof slate roof had been put on. Because of this roof, the fire went undetected for some time. In fighting the fire, knife-sharp pieces from the roof kept the firefighters from getting close enough to aggressively fight the fire.

South and North Halls of St. Johnsbury Academy were lost to fire. South Hall was lost on January 11, 1926. Luckily, the fifteen who lived there escaped

The Methodist church, 1915.

YMCA building. *From* Street, Public Buildings and General Views of St. Johnsbury, Vermont, *published by F.O. Clark.*

uninjured. Shortly after firemen arrived near 6:00 a.m., the fire was beyond being contained. The north wall collapsed within forty-five minutes and the remaining three were toppled within the hour. March 1956 saw a similar fate to the North Hall. Walls that were over two feet thick with an inside cavity allowed the fire to spread quickly from one location to another, and although the brick walls survived, the building was lost. Students managed to work below and save athletic equipment, musical instruments and books.

November 26, 1966, was a sad day for the town when Notre Dame de Victoire Church was lost in a fire that was set intentionally by a young boy with the help of a candle. A landmark seen from many a vista was lost from the landscape. The Catholic community suffered another loss by fire when the Catholic convent was destroyed by fire in 1972. This was also the same year that the then silent buildings of the old Fairbanks scale works were reduced to ashes by a fire on March 21. Despite efforts from local and surrounding town firemen, the main buildings were smoldering ashes by nightfall. Many of these buildings represented the talents of Lambert Packard, the company's architect, hired in 1866.

June 18, 1984, saw another of Lambert Packard's designs destroyed by fire. This was the YMCA building on Eastern Avenue, given by Henry Fairbanks. This was arson at its worst, resulting in the loss of yet another town landmark. Disaster struck Railroad Street again in 2000. In February of that year, the Daniels Block was lost, as were the lives of three men. The last victims of a house fire were on Boynton Avenue in 2003, when a popular art teacher in Waterford lost her life trying to save her aunt.

On September 5, 1998, St. Johnsbury fireman Eugene McDonough lost his life in the line of duty at a fire at a warehouse at the PMI building in Lyndonville. Responding to a mutual aid call on Engine Co. 3, Gene was killed when he returned to open the doors of the warehouse that had closed after he had already opened them. A portion of the wall above the door collapsed on him. Gene is the only St. Johnsbury firefighter to lose his life in the line of duty. A memorial is held every year at the firehouse on the weekend preceding the anniversary of the PMI fire. A monument sits outside the firehouse, reminding all of the supreme sacrifice that Gene made.

Just prior to the final editing of this history, another major fire left a big hole on Main Street beginning the evening of July 9, 2009. Nineteen tenants were displaced but no lives were lost. Damage was from the Christian Scientist Church south to the Passumpsic Bank. The three blocks in between were of brick fronts, and the four-story one in the middle was a total loss. Known as the old Masonic Block, it was designed by Lambert Packard, and Norman Atwood described it as being "with many divisions of design horizontally

F.W. Baptist Church (now Christian Scientist), Masonic Hall (second one from church) and Passumpsic Savings Bank (third from Church). *From* Street, Public Buildings and General Views of St. Johnsbury, Vermont, *published by F.O. Clark.*

and vertically, exhibiting Packard's preferences in windows and brickwork." At the top, a row of round-topped windows provided light for a banquet and lodge room in its former life. At the end of its life, the street entrance had been the Convenient One, a store "convenient" to all who lived and worked on Main Street. The Roach Block to the left was empty and the Walker Block to the right housed a bread store and Kennedy's Jewelry. Both of these blocks had been severely altered over the years. The Passumpsic Bank, a brick building also designed by Packard, survived, but not without smoke and water damage. Many fire departments joined St. Johnsbury firefighters in containing the fire to just that portion of Main Street.

# Floods

Three rivers—the Moose, Passumpsic and Sleepers—were a great source of power to the early settlers, but they have proven very problematic when they have risen too high and raged out of control, taking anything in their path. Such was the case with an early flood in September 1828; between the Sleepers and the west branch of the Passumpsic, five bridges were lost.

A sawmill, gristmill and carding machine were lost, as well as a building belonging to E. & T. Fairbanks. The high water of 1866 took the bridge across the Passumpsic at the Center Village, two bridges on the Moose and one on the Sleepers River. East of the railroad station, the dam on the Passumpsic was lost, causing the shutdown of the Nutt File Factory, Miller Carriage and other shops.

In the flood of 1869, the bridge at the Center survived, having been built higher after the 1866 flood, even though the floodwaters were two and a half feet higher than any former record. This deluge did, however, flood streets and houses and railroad tracks were washed away. The Sleepers River raised havoc with the Fairbanks scale works, washing away bridges, machinery and buildings.

And then came the flood of 1927—Vermont's worst yet. November 3 and 4 still live on in many senior citizens' memories, as the waters rose to record highs. At one point, the water in the Passumpsic River rose eleven inches in an hour. St. Johnsbury had sixty-two bridges when the flood struck and lost fourteen, all over forty feet long. Perhaps one of the most memorable scenes was the Hastings Bridge, which broke loose and floated like a big barge toward the Arlington Bridge (Paddocks Village). Hastings crashed into it, and both were totally lost, leaving only one bridge—Portland Street—to connect.

Hastings Bridge afloat, heading for Arlington Bridge, in the 1927 flood.

It was thought that the Maine Central Railroad Bridge had been weakened by the floodwaters and would probably succumb and take out the highway bridge, so the railroad bridge was deliberately burned down. St. Mary Street was hit hardest but sections of Elm Street, Concord Avenue, Passumpsic Street, Bay Street and upper Railroad Street were also inundated. Houses on Main Street in St. Johnsbury Center saw the worst losses, as most were lifted right off their foundations. This time the Center bridge was washed downstream; parts were salvaged and the bridge was put back in rapid time. The Arlington Bridge was a local one and would not be finished until May 1928; in the meantime, a footbridge was erected, but vehicles had to go via Portland Street and Concord Avenue.

Other problems included the loss of water from Stiles Pond to those west of the Passumpsic River due to a break in the fourteen-inch water pipe. The *Caledonian-Record* put out a single sheet paper by way of a hand press for four days. The Fairbanks factory was back in operation after ten days of major repair and cleanup. The Maine Central set up a temporary station at Cary Maple Sugar Company because of the burning of the bridge. It provided the only rail service to get food into the town, as the Canadian Pacific and the St. J. and L.C. Railroad had suffered major damage. The Maine Central had constructed an emergency replacement bridge within a week; needless to say,

The intentional burning of the railroad bridge on Portland Street, 1927 flood.

this was round-the-clock work. Many organizations, such as the Red Cross, banded together to make sure that victims of the flood were taken care of.

Waters would not reach such high levels again until June 1973. Widespread flooding occurred after two days of heavy rain. In June 2002, the Passumpsic reached 19.12 feet, its highest reading since the flood of 1973. A wet May had left the ground saturated when June 11 and 12 saw 3.46 inches that pushed the river out of its banks.

## Other Weather Happenings

When conversation stalls, one can always talk about the weather, and up here one doesn't really have to wait too long before the weather changes, giving one plenty to talk about! One weather event in St. Johnsbury was the Hurricane of 1938, which was the first hurricane to strike our town in full fury. September 21 saw the storm come right up the river valley. Claire Dunne Johnson, in her volume II of *I See by the Paper*, writes that the storm was responsible for "bringing us three unforgettable hours of winds up to 75 m.p.h. Trees and power lines went down early in the evening, and it was an eerie experience, sitting in a house lighted only by a few candles, and hearing the sounds outside as trees cracked and fell everywhere." Around seventy-five trees and limbs came down in the village, causing substantial damage but relatively few injuries.

Edward Fairbanks mentions a couple of weather happenings in 1870. During the summer, there were thunderstorms nearly every day. July 20 saw the mercury at one hundred degrees in the shade. On October 20, the community was shaken by an earthquake, "the most violent shake ever known in the town." The South Church steeple swayed and the brick Union School rocked but little damage was done—although nerves were really shaken! The various changes in a short time in January 1878 are reported by Fairbanks: pansies were blossoming in gardens on the Plain and sap was running on the hillsides but by the middle of the month the mercury had dipped to twenty-two, thirty and forty degrees below zero.

Mark Breen, meteorologist at the Fairbanks Museum, shared some of the more recent weather extremes. The weather records at the museum date back to 1894.

1969. February 25–28, greatest snowstorm. A nor'easter buried St. Johnsbury with thirty-six inches of snow, setting a state record for the most snow in twenty-four hours (thirty-three inches).

1977. July 20–21, hot! Hottest weather since 1919, St. Johnsbury at 99 degrees both days.

1979. February, long cold spell. Three weeks in a row, morning temperatures were below 0. The coldest mornings were February 12 and 13, when St. Johnsbury saw negative 32 degrees.

1998. Warmest year on record, with St. Johnsbury's average temperature at 47.6 degrees

2001. Deepest snow on April 1 (no joke): twenty-seven inches at 7:00 a.m.

2004. January, coldest daylight since 1917. Temperatures stayed at 7 below zero or colder for sixty hours from January 14 to January 16.

2007. Snowiest December on record—53.7 inches.

2007. Valentine's Day Blizzard: 20 to 30 inches was common.

2007–08. Snowiest winter on record—139.2, beating 1968–69 by 0.2 inches.

2008. Wettest summer on record—20.07 inches of rain fell from June 1 to August 31, including 9.16 inches of rain in July (wettest July on record).

2008. Wettest year on record. St. Johnsbury broke the 50-inch mark for the total rain and melted snow measured for the year. Total 50.47, compared to an average of 38.54 inches.

Above are the records to be broken in the future, which will stir more conversation. Closing out the weather segment in this chapter is the year 1924, when "Snowflake" Bentley came to St. Johnsbury and spoke to the Brotherhood meeting at the Methodist church. Wilson was his first name, and he hailed from Jericho, Vermont. His presentation included slides of his work. His pictures of snowflakes opened eyes to the beauty of each and every different snowflake, providing yet another prospect on the weather.

# CHAPTER 11

# ST. JOHNSBURY NOW

## Fairbanks Scales

In Chapter 3, we saw the E. & T. Fairbanks Company come into being and success established with the invention of the platform scale. It is now known as the Fairbanks Scales, with corporate facilities in Kansas City, Missouri. It has been a privately owned corporation since 1988. It has manufacturing facilities in St. Johnsbury, consisting of light-capacity product manufacturing, engineering and administrative offices. Heavy-capacity product manufacturing, engineering and administrative offices are in Meridian, Mississippi. There are customer support systems nationwide. How did we get to this point? In 1882, more than eighty thousand scales were being produced yearly. In 1897, the company offered two thousand standard varieties and made thousands of different models, which were distributed by a network of company agents and semi-independent distributors. One of these was Fairbanks-Morse & Company.

Charles Hosmer Morse was born in St. Johnsbury Center, nephew of Zelotus Hosmer, one of the first salesmen for the scale company. In 1850, at the young age of seventeen, Charles apprenticed himself for three years, working in the Boston and New York offices as well. In 1857, he was sent to Chicago, and in 1866, he opened the first office of Fairbanks-Morse & Company in Cincinnati. This company would overshadow the E. & T. Fairbanks plant and eventually gain control in 1916. In 1927, with New York offices becoming part of Fairbanks-Morse, they had complete control. Morse did not confine himself to scales, adding windmills, pumps and other industrial equipment while gaining control. The late 1950s saw Fairbanks-Morse merge with Penn-Texas, and the company was renamed Fairbanks-Whitney. The 1960s saw Fairbanks-Whitney rebrand itself as Colt Industries, Fairbanks Weighing Division; next was the relocation of the St. Johnsbury plant to Route 2 east, also in the 1960s. The 1970s saw the relocation of heavy-capacity weighing machines to Meridian. The year 1988 saw Fancor, Inc., headed by Bill Norden, acquire Fairbanks from Colt, which brings us to the present.

## Weidmann Electrical Technology

In 1877, Heinrich Weidmann started an industry in Switzerland, manufacturing pressboard for the textile industry. In 1971, EHV Weidmann Inc., now Weidmann Electrical Technology, came to St. Johnsbury and located on what was the former Cobb farm on Route 5 north before the country club. This company produces transformer board insulation materials, fabricated components and complete insulation systems for electrical transformers and industrial equipment. Today, Weidmann is the most significant global supplier of electrical insulation for the power transformer market. It is one of St. Johnsbury's top employers.

## Northeastern Vermont Regional Hospital

Valentine's Day 1972 saw the opening of Northeastern Vermont Regional Hospital (NVRH), taking over the duties of St. Johnsbury and Brightlook Hospitals. A committee was formed in 1963 to study the healthcare needs of the community. As a result of this study, it was decided to build a new facility. A public fund drive was started in 1968, with its goal of $800,000 reached in January of the following year. The new hospital is located just north of town on Hospital Drive on the grounds of the former 110-acre Grapes family farm. It was designed by the Burlington architectural firm of Freeman, French and Freeman and constructed by Vermont Construction Company of Laval, Quebec. When this one-hundred-bed facility opened, it boasted of three emergency rooms, two X-ray rooms and four post-anesthesia rooms, something that had not been available before. Another plus was ample parking and, perhaps the most important element, room to expand! An interesting part of this whole transition project was "Operation Transplant," which was a plan begun five years before concerning the moving of patients and equipment to the new site. It was a schedule that assigned daily tasks to the twenty-eight departments and coordinated with the other departments. The goal was to be ready a week before the actual transition. This move saw differences in communication, a much more elaborate switchboard plus the new beeper-call system, where hospital personnel would wear lapel receivers; they could receive a signal up to twenty miles away.

The complex has grown and includes medical office buildings and St. Johnsbury Health and Rehabilitation, a 110-bed facility across the road. Sherman Drive was constructed to give access to new buildings. Buildings included an office and fracture clinic of Dr. Richard Gagnon; another houses the physical therapy center. Additional lots were leased to Caledonia Home Health Agency, Inc., in 1987. In 1990, an umbrella administrative agency named Northern Counties Health Care, Inc., would oversee Caledonia Home Health, hospice and health centers around the Northeast. In 1994, buildings were constructed for the CALEX Emergency Services. This provided for vehicles as well as personnel and a helipad for airlifting patients to other hospitals.

At the foot of Hospital Drive is the Bloch Building, owned by NVRH, which houses the Norris Cotton Cancer Center–North. At the present time, a dialysis center has just started serving patients in the area. This is located in the Bloch Building as well.

## Catamount Arts

Catamount Arts was founded in 1975, its mission being to broaden the cultural climate of Vermont and New Hampshire through the offerings of film, theatre, music, dance and visual arts. This organization rented and operated out of the old post office building on Eastern Avenue. The post office had been built in 1936 and served as such until it was moved to Main Street in 1963. In this facility, Catamount had a one-hundred-seat film center and limited space for art showings. Entertainers and shows were brought to the community through this organization.

Next door at the Masonic temple, things were not going well. Enrollment had drastically declined, and heating and maintenance costs were harder and harder to cover. The temple had been built in 1912 for $35,000 by Freemasons. It was the largest Masonic temple in all of New England and it boasted twenty thousand people at its grand opening. The Masons sought help from a nonprofit that could use the basement and street levels and allow them to continue their activities on the third floor. An agreement was reached that turned the space over to Catamount for free, but Catamount was responsible for raising funds for renovations.

Raising $1.3 million was achieved by soliciting businesses, a capital campaign and loans through local banks. The St. Johnsbury Academy

The former post office and Masonic temple on Eastern Avenue.

building trades department did the majority of the work. The original woodwork was preserved and restored, including original hardwood floors. The basement was restored to include office space as well as a one-hundred-seat live performance space called the Catamount Cabaret. There are two new theatres, and an elevator provides access for all. Once again, designers sought to maintain the historic characteristics of this building, and it now has a new life and certainly broadens the cultural atmosphere of St. Johnsbury. This whole project was revealed to the public in October 2008.

## St. Johnsbury

The town has a very rich history and continues to support its roots while still moving into the twenty-first century. St. Johnsbury Chamber of Commerce promotes St. Johnsbury's marketing and development. The Northeast Kingdom Chamber of Commerce promotes the area and surrounding businesses. Both have websites and clearly do a great job in promoting St. Johnsbury. There will be bumps in the road, but they have always risen to the occasion, whether it was saving the St. Johnsbury House, keeping the Fairbanks Company in St. Johnsbury, saving the North Church tower or maintaining old buildings for new uses—residents are committed.

# BIBLIOGRAPHY

Beck, Richard. *A Proud Tradition a Bright Future*. N.p.: R.R. Dunnelley & Son, Co., 1992.

Fairbanks, Edward T. *The Town of St. Johnsbury Vt.* St. Johnsbury, VT: Cowles Press, 1914.

Fairbanks Scales. *175 Years of Excellence*. 175th anniversary booklet, 2005.

Heon, Gerald. Scrapbooks of St. Johnsbury. St. Johnsbury, VT.

Horton, Charles H. *Poems by Charles H. Horton*. St. Johnsbury, VT: Cowles Press, 1925.

Johnson, Claire Dunne. *Images of America St. Johnsbury*. Dover, NH: Arcadia Publishing, 1996.

———. *I See by the Paper…* St. Johnsbury, VT: Cowles Press, 1987.

———. *I See by the Paper…* Vol. II. St. Johnsbury, VT: Cowles Press, 1989.

Kenny, Kathleen M.; James B. Peterson, PhD; John G. Crock, PhD; Geoffrey A. Mandel; and Chris K. Slesar. *Life and Death in the Northeast Kingdom: Archaeology and History at the Old Burial Ground in St. Johnsbury, Vermont, CA. 1790–1853*. Consulting Archaeology Program, University of Vermont Report No. 303. April 2003.

Mitchell, Mark D. *St. Johnsbury Athenaeum Handbook of the Art Collection*. Lunenburg, VT: Stinehour Press, 2005.

Smith, Lowell. *150th Anniversary of the Founding of St. Johnsbury Vermont 1937.* St. Johnsbury, VT: Cowles Press, n.d.

Stone, Arthur Fairbanks. *Old Time Stories of St. Johnsbury Vermont.* St. Johnsbury, VT: Caledonian Record, 1938.

———. *St. Johnsbury Illustrated.* St. Johnsbury, VT: Caledonian Press—C.M. Stone & Company, 1891.

*Streets, Public Buildings and General Views of St. Johnsbury, Vermont.* Gardner, MA: F.O. Clark, Lithotype Printing and Publishing Co., n.d.

Thompson, Zadock. *History of Vermont, Natural, Civil, and Statistical.* Burlington, VT: Chauncy Goodrich, 1842.

Trustees of St. Johnsbury Academy. *An Historical Sketch of St. Johnsbsury Academy 1842–1922.* N.p., n.d.

*The Vermonter* 27, no. 9 (1922).

Visit us at
www.historypress.net

CPSIA information can be obtained
at www.ICGtesting.com
Printed in the USA
BVHW041134101218
535246BV00005B/28/P

9 781540 218858